Current Developments
in Language Testing

Applied Language Studies
Edited by David Crystal

Current Developments in Language Testing

Edited by

Arthur Hughes and Don Porter

Department of Linguistic Science
University of Reading, UK

1983

Academic Press

A Subsidiary of Harcourt Brace Jovanovich, Publishers

London · New York
Paris · San Diego · San Francisco · São Paulo
Sydney · Tokyo · Toronto

ACADEMIC PRESS INC. (LONDON) LTD.
24/28 Oval Road
London NW1

United States Edition published by
ACADEMIC PRESS INC.
111 Fifth Avenue
New York, New York 10003

British Library Cataloguing in Publication Data

Current developments in language testing.—(Applied
language studies)
1. Grading and marking (Students)   2. Modern
languages—Study and teaching
I. Hughes, Arthur   II. Porter, Don
III. Series
418   PB35

ISBN: 0-12-360880-5
LCCCN: 83 70949

Phototypeset by Oxford Publishing Services
Printed in Great Britain by
T. J. Press (Padstow) Ltd., Padstow

Contributors

J. Charles Alderson
Institute for English Language Education, Bowland College,
University of Lancaster, Lancaster LA1 4YT

Brendan J. Carroll
Pergamon Institute of English, 8 Manor Place, Speen, Newbury,
Berks RG13 1RB

Alan Davies
Department of Linguistics, University of Edinburgh, 14 Buccleuch Place,
Edinburgh 8

Andrew Harrison
35 Brentham Way, Ealing, London W5 1BE

Arthur Hughes
Department of Linguistic Science, University of Reading, Whiteknights,
Reading RG6 2AA

Keith Morrow
Bell Educational Trust, Old House, Church Lane, Eaton,
Norwich NR4 6NW

John W. Oller, Jr.
Department of Linguistics, University of New Mexico, Albuquerque,
New Mexico 87131

Brian Parkinson
Department of Education, University of Stirling, Stirling FK9 4LA

Don Porter
Centre for Applied Language Studies, Language Resource Centre,
University of Reading, Whiteknights, Reading RG6 2AP

Ian Seaton
The British Council, 10 Spring Gardens, London SW1A 2BN

Bernard Spolsky
Department of English, Bar-Ilan University, Ramat-Gan, Israel

A. H. Urquhart
University of Aston in Birmingham, Gosta Green, Birmingham B4 7ET

Helmut J. Vollmer
*Universität Osnabrück, Fachbereich 7, Kommunikation/Ästhetik,
Postfach 4469, D-4500 Osnabrück, West Germany*

Anthony Woods
*Department of Applied Statistics, University of Reading, Whiteknights,
Reading RG6 2AA*

Preface

The recent past has seen three important developments in language testing. The first of these has been a greatly increased level of research directed at investigating the structure of foreign language ability, much of it stemming from Oller's heretical suggestion that language competence might not be divisible in the way that a generation of language testers had assumed. The second has been the debate about how to devise reliable and valid measures of communicative (rather than purely grammatical) competence. The third has been the growing number of tests designed to test not general language ability but language for specific purposes such as the study of engineering in Britain, etc.

These three developments provided the themes for a seminar held under the auspices of the British Association for Applied Linguistics, at Reading University in December 1981. It was felt that the time was ripe for a careful consideration of the progress that had been made in each. Accordingly, for each of the themes a keynote paper and at least one formal response were invited, as well as reports of current research and development. It was intended from the outset that these would form the basis for a publication in order to reach a wider audience than could be at Reading. For the participants, the seminar proved to be a very profitable and enjoyable experience. Its success was due in no small measure to the quality of papers that were presented. We are grateful to the participants for allowing us to publish a selection of those papers here, and are particularly grateful to John Oller who, though he did not attend the meeting, very kindly agreed to make a response to the keynote paper on the structure of language proficiency.

September, 1983　　　　　　　　　　　　　　　　　　　　Arthur Hughes
Reading　　　　　　　　　　　　　　　　　　　　　　　　Don Porter

Contents

SECTION I

The structure of language proficiency

1

Keynote paper

The structure of foreign language competence

Helmut J. Vollmer

In the recent past, competing hypotheses about second language ability have been put forward based on differing assumptions as to the nature and structure of linguistic and communicative competence, namely the multi-dimensional model as opposed to the one-dimensional model. It has been claimed for both models that they are theoretically plausible and that they are backed up by more or less strong empirical evidence. In the meantime, much discussion has been going on internationally and, equally important, substantial research results have been presented. In addition, the methodological aspects of the issue have been elaborated upon and new theoretical advances have been proposed with the effect that no firm answer appears possible in the near future to the question: "What exactly is the structure of foreign language ability?" But at least there does appear to be a clear answer now to the question of whether or not it makes sense to assume that only one single unitary factor of language competence really exists. The answer is "no" or, to put it in Oller's words, "the strongest form of the unitary hypothesis was wrong" (Oller, 1983d). The strong position once taken by Oller and his associates has recently been funda-mentally revised.

I would not go as far as to assert that the issue of a general language proficiency (GLP) "is essentially a non-issue theoretically", as Alan Davies put it during a language testing conference at Lancaster in 1980 (Davies, 1982:181). But certainly it has changed its quality and lost some of its forcefulness as a research question: the discussion has, in my view, somehow led away from the macro-level of mathematical data reduction procedures to a psychologically more informed and better motivated infor-

DVLPMNTS IN LANGUAGE TESTING
ISBN: 0-12-360880-5

mation processing view of language performance and to the intensive analysis of tasks and of individual differences on a micro-level of behaviour, including a neurofunctional perspective. Others will probably place more stress on the fact that both levels and approaches are necessary, both can stand in their own right, and the two are even complementary in the study of language competence. The reason I have myself spoken in the past of a shift in focus has to do, of course, with my own subjective judgement that I would consider any factor analytic study (of whatever kind) to be of little value until we have more closely investigated and understood the *nature* of foreign language ability and how it relates to language performance. I hope that my preference will become reasonably clear as I go on.

The title of this paper was originally "The Unitary Competence Hypothesis" (UCH); I have changed it to what it is now as this seems to be a better indication of the general problem at issue facing everyone in the language testing field today, irrespective of the competence model favoured. It is the problem of the validity of the tests developed or used and especially the problem of how their assumed construct validity can best be demonstrated. The evidence on which the UCH was based was not as clear-cut or as strong as was suggested. Likewise, those in favour of a multi-dimensional model of linguistic competence also seemed to rely on rather questionable arguments in the past. The aim of this paper is therefore manifold:

1. to give a brief historical overview of the central issue,
2. to present some theoretical as well as empirical arguments for and against different models of foreign language competence (as these have been put forward until recently),
3. to describe the "state of the art" as I see it now,
4. to outline some perspectives as they are likely to develop.

It should be made clear from the start that I shall try to be as balanced as possible; especially when it comes to points (3) and (4) I cannot but rely heavily on my own subjective judgement and evaluation.

Throughout the paper I shall restrict myself as much as possible to the analysis of *foreign* or *second* language competence. The relationship between L1 and L2 abilities, although always implicitly present as a largely unresolved problem, will be dealt with specifically only at certain points. The concept of foreign language *aptitude* (whether it has any equivalent in psychological reality or not) will also be left out of my considerations altogether (but see Carroll (1981) for an excellent historical and theoretical account). The same will be the case for the construct of a *language acquisition device* as postulated and discussed anew by Chomsky and others (cf. Chomsky, 1980a and b).

In this paper I shall make a clear distinction between foreign language *proficiency* and language *ability* (or abilities). The latter notion will be used as a synonym for *"competence"* thus referring to a *dynamic* construct. It includes aspects of *implicit knowledge* of rules (defined as consolidations of prior mental experiences and information stored) just as much as *basic cognitive operations* being more or less consciously carried out. *Skills*, for example, are considered to be acquired routines, forming a subsytem within the overall structure of human abilities. They are automatized processes, carried out subconsciously, cognitive or sensory-motor in nature, yet being a definite part of the domain-specific ability system. *Plans* and *strategies* on the other hand are thought of as constituting more or less conscious mental actions. The notion of strategy seems to be of particular relevance for the study of foreign language competence since it denotes a specific subset of cognitive procedures which the learner has to apply (in terms of constructing alternative plans) whenever he cannot solve the problem at hand or reach the goal set by way of applying the knowledge and skills which he has available.

All of the different aspects and levels of foreign language ability are thought of as representing acquired yet provisional dispositions and individual qualities governing the execution of mental activities in general and the performance of L2 achievements in particular.

One more word concerning the notion *"language proficiency"*. In the literature it is used in two different senses. One pertains to the *performance level* and relates then to the extent and adequacy of the learner's control of the (foreign) language in all kinds of situations and social interactions as demonstrated in tests. The other meaning unjustifiedly jumps over to the *construct or competence level* as is the case when proficiency is defined as the "degree of competence" of a learner or as "the capability in a given language demonstrated by an individual at a given point in time independent of a specific textbook, chapter in the book or pedagogical method" (Brière, 1972:322; cf. also Spolsky, 1973:175 or Oller, 1979:16 for a definition of "proficiency" on the construct level). Unfortunately, these two levels are sometimes mixed in the discussion of the problem at hand. In accordance with classical test theory, however, it goes without saying that the measurement level and what is derived from it or assumed to be conveyed by it should be kept strictly apart. Throughout my paper I shall try to maintain this distinction.

Understanding theoretically what is to be tested or has been tested is absolutely essential in the testing business. We shall therefore have to concern ourselves more with the validation of our tests or at least strive for a greater balance between the principles of reliability and validity (of any sort). In other words, what we need is to move away from psychometric preoccupation to a more comprehensive, applied linguistic approach in testing.

I shall now turn to a brief historical and theoretical overview of the issue in question.

Historical and theoretical overview

Non-unitary models of foreign language competence

Due to the strong influence of the linguistic theory of structuralism it was for a long time accepted without much discussion that, basically, knowing a language meant knowing its elements and having mastered (by way of habitualization and automatization) different modes of putting them to use. Accordingly, after the work of Fries and especially Lado, it seemed to be a shared theoretical view that foreign language ability consisted of several aspects. These were thought to be identical with the dimensions of achievement in a foreign language which in turn could be related to a performance matrix. A matrix of this kind usually combined the elements of a language to be mastered (defined as "simple skills") with the integrated use of different levels of knowledge in solving complex language tasks (defined as "integrated skills"). It was used as a framework in attempting to define linguistic competence in operational terms along the lines of a multi-dimensional approach and for test construction. Theoretically, at least, it was considered to be possible to develop a valid and reliable test for each of the cells. In practice, however, it was agreed that it would be senseless to obtain all these different measures. This would be carrying the process of analysis too far, it was argued.

The important point here is that it was only *implicitly* assumed by the proponents of this multi-dimensional approach that each of the cells in the matrix is related to an underlying competence, being more or less independent of others. This theoretical position—though considered to be somewhat self-evident—has never been formulated explicitly by anyone in its strong form (that is: 16 cells = 16 competencies), nor in its weak form (4 integrated skills = 4 competencies), as far as I know. Carroll (1968) was the one to come closest when suggesting his chart of linguistic competences and that of linguistic performance abilities (all based on underlying competencies). But even in Carroll's work we do not find a clear verbalization of the divisible competence hypothesis either in its strong or in any weaker form as the guiding structural assumption of his research (for a closer discussion of Carroll's multi-dimensional approach for measuring foreign language proficiency cf. Vollmer 1981a or Vollmer and Sang, 1983).

From the point of view of classical test theory it was argued that the degree of mastery in a foreign language could be inferred from the multitude of measured language performances (at least four). Thus it would be possible to form some sort of overall picture of a person's language ability and (by way of generalization) of his ability to act in a more or less predictable manner even in future situations requiring language use (including those which cannot be foreseen). Therefore, a large variety of tests were designed, each one purporting to measure a different aspect of language performance, each one supposedly adding information as to the structure and the degree of development of a learner's foreign language "knowledge" or "competence". These tests were then combined with each other in different ways constituting specific batteries for measuring language proficiency, each one of which was considered to be highly valid. Examples are such instruments as the TOEFL (Educational Testing Service, 1964 ff.), the ELBA (Ingram, 1964) and the EPTB (Davies, 1964 and later). As Davies has noted with irony: "It was always recognized that the sum of the whole was greater than any one of the parts" (1978:216). A test battery provides us with a score for each sub-test (which can be given different weights if so desired); it also gives a total score, thereby providing an additive and integrative description of a person's language command as a whole covering all the areas of performance included.

Astonishingly enough it always seemed to be accepted at the same time that there would, of course, be some degree of interrelationship among the different performances measured.

In fact, it almost went without saying that in statistical analysis some sort of common factor would normally appear on which many—if not all—of the tests included would have some loading. The declared aim of test construction, however, was to reach reliability coefficients as high as possible and keep the intercorrelations among the tests at a minimum. A general factor, explaining most (or at least a substantial amount) of the common variance among the different test measures was indeed never thought of. It was not provided for in classical test theory. Even if a strong first factor did show up it tended to be neglected: it was simply of no central interest in comparison with the additional common factors and certainly did not lead to a revision of the divisible competence position (cf. Carroll, 1975, as a good example of this).

In sum, the theoretical claim for some multi-dimensional approach—even though this lacked a clear articulation—and also many of the psychological arguments put forward seemed rather plausible for what they were (as was the case with some of the arguments in favour of the UCH): they partly depended on what was available as linguistic, psycholinguistic or psychometric theory at the time of formulation.

With the introduction of the "communicative competence" notion and the beginning of functional testing we find that assumptions concerning the nature and structure of foreign language ability (all of them non-unitary!) are now for the first time being stated more or less explicitly. This is true, to some extent, with Canale and Swain (1980), for example. After reviewing all the relevant literature they feel that it is unlikely that communicative competence could be reduced to only one global language proficiency dimension. They postulate instead (at least) three different dimensions of communicative competence in their theoretical framework: grammatical competence, sociolinguistic competence, and strategic competence. As plausible as this model may be, it immediately invites a number of modifications, expansions, deletions, rearrangements, etc., all of which are open to discussion; that is to say, the framework is still highly tentative, and is not yet based on any empirical investigation. The empirical testing of this model (at least in part) is under way, however (Canale, 1983). The work of Canale and Swain has influenced several other researchers already in trying to define communicative competence more clearly (however provisionally) before partially testing it out within a multitrait–multimethod approach. Among those who have been influenced by Canale and Swain are Bachman and Palmer (1980, 1981). Canale and Swain's overall model differs from that of the latter two writers in so far as the former postulates communicative competence within each of the skill areas to be made up of four sub-dimensions (linguistic, sociolinguistic and pragmatic competence as well as fluency). So far Bachman and Palmer have concentrated on the overall skill level; they have started out by (only) hypothesizing two independent foreign language abilities, one for speaking, one for reading (cf. again Bachman and Palmer, 1981, for their way of defining these constructs in theoretical and operational terms).

As convincing as the research results of Bachman and Palmer are (see Empirical findings, in this paper), what irritates me most (in the papers that I know of) is the half-heartedness of their psychological reasoning as well as the almost complete lack of interpretation of their data in any meaningful theoretical perspective. Why exactly should *speaking* and *reading* be *different mental activities* based on differing abilities? And why did they choose speaking (not writing) and reading (not listening comprehension)? Perhaps only for practical reasons? To be sure, the authors clearly state their hypothesis in advance but what do the two factors found really mean in substance other than "communicative competence in reading" and "communicative competence in speaking"?

The development of the UCH

In trying to reconstruct the theoretical basis for the assumption of a unitary competence in all language users we should turn back to the end of the sixties when Spolsky asked: "What does it mean to know a language or how do you get someone to perform his competence?" (Spolsky, 1973). One of his main points was that knowledge of a language means knowing its rules.

> Knowing a language is a matter of having mastered (as yet incompletely specified) rules; the ability to handle new sentences is evidence of knowing the rules that are needed to generate them. (Spolsky, 1973:173)

Spolsky thus reminded us of "two vital truths about language, the fact that language is redundant, and the fact that it is creative" (1973:167). In his approach knowledge of a language, being a matter of knowledge of rules, seemed much the same as *"underlying linguistic competence"*. This competence operates in all the different kinds of performances, be they active or passive (the latter being an equally creative process on the part of the learner).

It is worth noting that Spolsky only speaks of an "underlying linguistic competence", not of a "unitary competence". In another context he considers knowledge of rules to be the "principal factor" (1973:174) in the understanding as well as in the production of messages (not the one and only factor explaining all sorts of language behaviour). This distinction is quite important. It becomes clearer when we follow Spolsky's suggestion that we could find out about "knowledge of a language" equally well when testing passive or active skills:

> This last does not of course mean that an individual's performance as a speaker is the same as his performance as a listener; such a claim would clearly be ridiculous, for it would be tantamount to saying that anyone who could read a Shakespeare play could also write it. All that it does claim is that the same linguistic competence, the same knowledge of rules, underlies both kinds of performance. (Spolsky, 1973:174)

This quotation clearly indicates the shift of focus that has taken place from the *differences* between the skills (and how they might relate to underlying competences) to what they might have *in common* by way of a shared basic competence stretching out into all the skills. It is not claimed (as yet) that all possible linguistic performances are based on one and only one single ability. To give an example: in trying to explain the ability to read (and understand!) a Shakespeare play or even write a play or a poem ourselves we will have to take other competencies (constructs) into account—distinct from and in addition to "knowledge of rules". If our focus of interest is concentrated on the assumed central linguistic competence (or that portion which may be common to the operation of all the skills), the additional cognitive forces—those which are not common to all the skills—do not disappear. They are simply out of focus for the time being. But Spolsky goes one step further by introducing the notion of *"overall proficiency"*. He argues that the autonomy of the different skills might not be as large as often assumed. The language learner in the course of language acquisition most probably does not develop a multitude of more or less related specific abilities, but rather a central, comprehensive and integrative linguistic competence which will pervade all forms of language use. This competence is identified with "overall language proficiency" (note that the term proficiency is used here on the construct level).

As far as I know Spolsky did not give any substantial explanation or justification for this theoretical position. On the contrary, he was careful enough not to speculate any further on this issue, which nevertheless seemed plausible. When asked at the 1974 Washington Language Testing Symposium for a clear definition of overall proficiency, Spolsky answered:

> It should be obvious by now that I can't say that precisely, or I would have. It's an idea that I'm still playing with. It has to correlate with the sum of various kinds of things in some way, because it should underlie any specific abilities. In other words, I have the notion that ability to operate in a language includes a good, solid central portion (which I'll call overall proficiency) plus a number of specific areas based on experience and which will turn out to be either the skill or certain sociolinguistic situations.
>
> (Jones and Spolsky, 1975:69)

It should be noted that Spolsky does not differentiate between L1 and L2 language acquisition. The same holds true for Oller.

In order to understand Oller's theoretical thinking, which led to the formulation of the UCH, we will have to concentrate on the central notion of an *"internalized expectancy grammar"*, which has been developed step by step in recent years (cf. Oller 1974, 1978, 1979). This concept is partly based on research results from cognitive psychology, especially on findings in perceptual psychology as these have been summarized and systematized by Neisser (1967), for example.

One of the basic notions in the description of the active and constructive role of the perceiver is that of "analysis-by-synthesis". This concept is supposed to characterize the cognitive activities on the part of a perceiver in the process of perceiving in general and decoding language specifically. The hearer is thought to be able to generate internally an equivalent for every incoming signal, analysing this by producing a rough synthesis (meaningful expectation) of his own which is then compared with the results of the exact analysis in a step-by-step procedure. This hypothesis has been extended by Oller to the productive side of language use which is designated accordingly "a kind of synthesis-by-analysis" (Oller, 1978:45). The idea is that the processes of generating a sequence of linguistic elements in terms of a meaningful utterance are governed by an overall plan or communicative intention ("synthesis") within a speaker/writer. This plan could be thought of as some kind of "executive control program" (Vigil and Oller, 1976) guiding and supervising all the operations and sub-routines in the process of producing language as part of social interaction. Both the hypothesis-building activities of a listener/reader in language comprehension and the activities of planning and monitoring of a speaker/writer in language production are considered by Oller to be based on the one "expectancy grammar".

What exactly is an "expectancy grammar"? It has been defined in short as "the learner's predictive competence in formal, functional and strategic terms" (Candlin, in the preface to Oller, 1979).

To put it in Oller's own words:

> The term 'expectancy grammar' calls attention to the peculiarly sequential organization of language in actual use. Natural language is perhaps the best known example of the complex organization of elements into sequences and classes, and sequences of classes which are composed of other sequences of classes and so forth. The term 'pragmatic expectancy grammar' further calls attention to the fact that the sequences of classes of elements, and hierarchies of them which constitute a language are available to the language user in real life situations because they are somehow indexed with reference to their appropriateness to extralinguistic contexts.
>
> In the normal use of language, no matter what level of language or mode of processing we think of, it is always possible to predict partially what will come next in any given sequence of elements. The elements may be sounds, syllables, words, phrases, sentences, paragraphs, or larger units of discourse. The mode of processing may be listening, speaking, reading, writing, or thinking, or some combination of these. In the meaningful use of language, some sort of pragmatic expectancy grammar must function in all cases.
>
> (Oller, 1979:24–25)

At another point the author stresses the dynamic character of his construct. At the same time the proficiency (measurement) and the ability (psychological construct) level are tacitly mixed and defined by one another.

> The notion of expectancy is introduced as a key to understand the nature of psychologically real processes that underlie language use. It is suggested that expectancy generating systems are constructed and modified in the course of language acquisition. Language proficiency is thus characterized as consisting of such an expectancy generating system. (Oller, 1979:16)

Oller's theoretical construct has been discussed in more detail and evaluated elsewhere (e.g. Sang and Vollmer, 1978; Vollmer and Sang, 1980). As for *second* or *foreign* language learning, it seems fair to say that the construct is broadly in accordance with 10 years of interlanguage research and even with an updated version of the interlanguage hypothesis as outlined by Selinker and Lamandella (1981). This holds true only for the general characterization of language acquisition as being a creative and constructive process, one to which the learner actively contributes by way of hypothesis building and testing, on the basis of what is already known and available to him and what he thus "expects". Yet the specific notion of *expectancy* as originally meant by Oller has been severely challenged in cognitive psychology within the last 10 years.

It was Neisser who in 1967 clearly stated the theory that perceptual processing could best be explained in terms of "analysis-by-synthesis". In 1976, however, he no longer believes that this can be taken literally:

> The anticipations of the listener, like those of the looker, are not highly specific. He does not know exactly what he will hear; otherwise why should he bother to listen? It would be a mistake to suppose that perceivers constantly formulate highly specific hypotheses about what is coming next and discard them in favor of better ones only when they fail to fit.
>
> (Neisser, 1976:28)

In one of his footnotes Neisser specifies that the concept of "analysis-by-synthesis" in the strict sense of the term can probably not be taken as an adequate description: "It would require that an implausibly large number of false hypotheses be generated all the time. The listener's active constructions must be more open and less specific, so that they are rarely disconfirmed" (1976:32). With regard to this change in position it seems very questionable indeed whether the construct of an internalized expectancy grammar supposed to be the deep centre of all language ability can be upheld. (I believe the term "expectancy" no longer plays a significant role in Oller's thinking).

From a theoretical point of view the notion of *general language proficiency* being the manifestation of an underlying competence and interpreted along the lines of an *expectancy grammar* has always been very vague, in my understanding at least. It could at best be taken as a handy formula or as a label indicating that foreign language ability has to do with the building up of a structured rule system (*grammar*) and with a constructive and creative role (*"expectancy"*) on the part of the learner (including "pragmatic mapping" activities, as Oller calls them). Is this much more than trivial? But what always escaped my insight was the claim that these cognitive and intellectual processes in foreign language acquisition that

Oller so rightly points to in his theory should be one-dimensional or *unitary*.

What was particularly irritating in the past was the fact that this position was repeated over and over again in its strong form with such alacrity, as if no doubts were possible at all. Apparently others have reacted similarly, for example Cummins (1979), who makes a distinction between a "convincing weak form and a less convincing strong form of Oller's arguments" (1979:198). Cummins points out that the difficulty with the strong position would be "immediately obvious when one considers that with the exception of severely retarded and autistic children, everybody acquires basic interpersonal communicative skills (BICS) in a first language (L1) regardless of IQ or academic aptitude. Also, the sociolinguistic aspects of communicative competence or functional language skills appear unlikely to be reducible to a global profiency dimension" :1979:198). (For a more detailed discussion see Oller (1983d) and also Cummins (1983). I must say that I never really understood why the interlanguage grammar of a foreign language should function "in a relatively integrated fashion in many communicative contexts" (Oller, 1983c) and why this should be the only and unitary source of individual differences.

The UCH has perhaps never been explained well enough in theoretical terms. The same, however, is true for any divisible competence model that has come to my awareness so far. It may well be that the formulation of the UCH in its strong form has influenced the proponents of other views to try to make their hypothesis more explicit. Even if the UCH were not correct and about to be abandoned by its most pronounced proponents (see An outline of "the state of the art"), it has certainly succeeded in forcing those claiming a divisible model of (foreign) language competence into serious re-consideration of their respective assumptions, thus having stimulated a period of fruitful controversy and international discussion which still continues. The UCH has been sharply criticized itself, not only on theoretical, but above all on empirical grounds as we shall see in the next section. It has largely served its (good) purpose.

Empirical findings (1965–1980/82)

In trying to summarize some of the most important findings as to the structure of foreign language ability one has to be aware, of course, that it is extremely difficult (if not impossible) to make a real comparison between different factorial studies. First of all, most of them (except the newer ones) have used factor analysis in a *merely exploratory* way. Secondly, they are based on widely divergent samples and variables. How do we know how the grammar test in one study relates to a similarly named test in another one? Thirdly, the different factors found, though in part labelled similarly, could mean different things in terms of factor loadings and in relation to the overall factorial structure which is specific for each single study. For these and other reasons a *comparative analysis* of the different studies over time will not be possible in the strict sense of the term. It seems to be of some interest, however, to get at least a suggestive overview of the number and chronology of the studies undertaken and of the results presented in the past with the intention of supporting either one of the two competing hypotheses. All the details (at least for the majority of the studies listed here) including number and nature of language tests included, sample being tested, method(s) of extraction and rotation used by the authors and conclusions being drawn by them, plus a critical re-assessment of their interpretations (partly based on a reanalysis of the data) have been given elsewhere (cf. Vollmer, 1980, or for a less compre-hensive presentation Sang and Vollmer, 1980 and Vollmer and Sang, 1983).

Remember that the strongest claim made by Oller and others said that the indivisibility hypothesis "allows only for a general component of test variance" (Oller, 1979:425), which means with no *additional* reliable variance accounted for by some of the remaining tests at least. From a methodological point of view it would have sufficed to present research results with at least two common factors (independent of their meaning) in order to disprove the correctness of the UCH. But from a theoretical standpoint this procedure *ex negativo* in favour of a multi-dimensional model (of whatever sort) would not bring us much further because it does not help in understanding the nature of foreign language competence any better. The same holds true vice-versa: if a multiple factor solution turns up as being the best fit to a set of data but cannot be interpreted in terms of the traditional integrated skills (strong form of the divisible competence hypothesis) or along the element dimensions of a language (weaker form of the hypothesis), it makes little sense to argue that therefore the named hypothesis has been convincingly disconfirmed—and thus the UCH has been supported. This is exactly what has been done by some of the proponents of the UCH (cf. Scholz *et al.*, 1980).

One last word concerning the different types of factor analysis used. Whenever *principal components* analysis had been applied by the original author as the only computatorial procedure, a *reanalysis* was done by my colleague, F. Sang and myself. The reason for this decision was based on the fact that principal components analysis seems to be particularly inade-quate as a method of testing the UCH. It tends to overestimate the weight and significance of the first factor by not partitioning the total amount of test variance into *common* variance, *test-specific* and *error variance.* In some of our reanalyses it could be shown that the application of *factor analysis* (normally with Varimax rotation) as opposed to principal components analysis could indeed change the factorial structure from a one-factor solution to a multiple-factor solution (cf. Vollmer and Sang, 1983). On the whole a more powerful statistical procedure for testing the hypotheses at stake has been called for by us and others, namely confirmatory factor analysis. In the meantime, this method has already been applied by researchers like Bachman and Palmer (1980, 1981) with striking results, as we shall see.

Table 1·1 only gives, as I have said, a suggestive overview of the number of factors found by the different authors and the labels they were given. I shall concentrate on only those factors that pertain to foreign language competence and that seem to be interpretable.

Table 1·1

	Author(s)	Factor(s)
1.	Gardner and Lambert (1965)	F1: Linguistic reasoning F2: French vocabulary knowledge F3 : Oral reading skill
2.	Reanalysis of Gardner and Lambert	F1: (Complex, but not general) F2: Speaking ability F3: Differential comprehension
3.	Löfgren (1969)	F1: Active knowledge of words and structures F2: Language fluency F3: Knowledge of structure F4: Word fluency F5: Passive vocabulary F6: Pronunciation
4.	Reanalysis of Löfgren (1969)	F1: Active knowledge of the language F2: Knowledge of grammar F3: Receptive competence F4: Fluency in (oral) expression F5: Fluency in pronunciation and at the word level
5.	Carroll (1975)	F1: General competence in French F2: Writing fluency F3: Speaking fluency F4: Pronunciation
6.	Reanalysis of Caroll (1975)	F1: General competence in French (except pronunciation)
7.	Oller (1976)	F1: General language proficiency
8.	Reanalysis of Oller (1976)	F1: Generalized foreign language competence
9.	Sang and Vollmer (1978)	F1: General (or at least) receptive competence

10.	Steltmann (1979)	F1: General factor of foreign language proficiency
11.	Reanalysis of Steltmann (1979)	F1: General factor
12.	Bonheim, Kreifelts, *et al.* (1979)	F1: Style F2: Vocabulary and reading comprehension F3: Grammar
13.	Reanalysis of Bonheim, Kreifelts *et al.* (1979)	F1: Style F2: Vocabulary F3: Grammar and reading comprehension
14.	Klein-Braley and Lück (1979)	F1: General language proficiency
15.	Reanalysis of Klein-Braley and Lück (1979)	F1: Elementary mastery of the L2 F2: Reading comprehension (Cloze)
16.	Reanalysis of Klein-Braley and Lück (1979) by Raatz (1980)	F1: (Passive) vocabulary and grammar (prepositions etc.) F2: Grammar F3: Cloze and translation (into English)
17.	Hosley and Meredith (1979)	F1: Global proficiency F2: Listening comprehension
18.	Reanalysis of Hosley and Meredith (1979)	F1: Receptive competence
19.	Snow and Hoefnagel-Höhle (1979)	F1: Phonological ability F2: Grammatical ability
20.	Oller and Hinofotis (1980)	F1: General language proficiency
21.	Reinterpretation of Oller and Hinofotis (1980)	F1: Oral interview ability F2: Comprehension
22.	Scholz *et al.* (1980)	F1: ? F2: Oral interview (method) F3: ? F4: Placement test (method)
23.	Reinterpretation of Scholz *et al.* (1980)	F1:) Unspecifiable F2:) multiple F3:) common F4:) factors

23a. It should be pointed out that Carroll (forthcoming) has also done some reanalysis and theorizing on Scholz *et al.* (1980).

24.	Bachman and Palmer (1980, 1981)	F1: Communicative competence in reading F2: Communicative competence in speaking
25.	Upshur and Homburg (1980)	<u>F1:</u>) A general factor F1:) can always be <u>F2:</u>) partitioned further (F1:)) into successively (F2:)) finer subfactors (F3:)) depending on the (F4:)) desired level of theorizing
26.	Vollmer (1980)	F1: Elementary knowledge F2: Complex comprehension (Data of Sang and Vollmer, 1978, with L1 abilities controlled for)
27.	Hughes and Woods (1982)	<u>F1:</u>) Number of components <u>F2:</u>) required to fit the data (F3:)) changes with groups: (F4:)) no interpretation given

28.	Sang (in preparation)	F1: Complex receptive competence in L1 and L2
		F2: Knowledge of single skills in L1 and L2
		F2: L2–specific knowledge of words; structure and global comprehension

As I have indicated, the "data" presented here can only be taken as the bare bones of living wholes. They have to be very carefully studied, each in its own context. But it can already be easily gathered, even on the basis of this incomplete information, that the empirical evidence for any one of the many hypotheses on foreign language competence is not overwhelmingly strong. The UCH in particular has suffered from severe criticism and could not be upheld.

An outline of "the state of the art"

I shall attempt now to sketch an overview of what might be called "the state of the art".

The psychological arguments as well as the empirical evidence presented over the past 10 years offer a by no means clear-cut basis for deciding in favour of any one of the theoretical positions posed. The structure of foreign language competence has not really become that much clearer in spite of all the efforts reported.

The main result of the vigorous research activity, especially during the past three years, seems to be that the strongest forms of both hypotheses can hardly be justified or upheld on the basis of the data available. Thus they both have to be rejected. In the case of the UCH this is publicly admitted now by one of its leading proponents. In a paper entitled "A Consensus for the '80s?" at the end of his 700-page book on "Issues in language testing research", Oller admits "that *the strongest form of the unitary hypothesis* was wrong" (Oller's emphasis). And he continues:

> The Bachman and Palmer research (Chapter 7, and references) as well as Carroll's theorizing and reanalysis of Scholz *et al.* (Chapter 4), has demonstrated conclusively that there exists a plurality of factors underlying language proficiency. Moreover, as Farhady (Chapter 2), and Upshur and Homburg (Chapter 9) have demonstrated, the existence of a plurality of factors can be empirically established by the computation of specificity estimates in keeping with classical psychometric theory even without the more powerful confirmatory factoring techniques employed by Bachman and Palmer, and by Purcell (Chapter 6).   (Oller Ed., 1983d)

On the other hand, many of the group factors found in the different studies cannot very easily be identified with either the postulated four integrated skills or the knowledge of specific elements or parts of a foreign language system. In particular, the traditional skill-by-component matrix apparently does not have a one-to-one equivalent on the ability level. The same seems to hold true for any of the enlarged multi-dimensional models of communicative competence such as that of Canale and Swain (1980) with its 40 cells ("dimensions" or at least "aspects" of foreign language ability).

A real comparison between the different studies presented is hardly possible, mainly because of differences in the sample, the number, choice and meaning of the variables included etc., but also because of differences in the linguistic, methodological and (test) theoretical background of the researchers involved. Nevertheless, some of the factors that show up more than once or even repeatedly (such as fluency, vocabulary, grammar, or some skill-related factors) may perhaps be taken as representing the same or at least a similar dimension of competence. But this is a highly controversial issue (non-similarity of the factorial structures as a whole out of which the named factors are isolated).

It cannot be denied that in a number of studies (either in the original form or after reanalysis) one single strong factor has emerged (Oller, 1976, Sang and Vollmer, 1978, Steltmann, 1979 or, in a sense, Carroll, 1975). This fact, however, could not very easily be interpreted along the lines of the UCH for several reasons, the main one being that the number of variables under consideration is insufficient in almost all of the studies mentioned. In other words, important aspects of language behaviour (above all the productive means of using a language) are not appropriately included for consideration. Moreover, the relatively small number of variables, highly correlated with each other, also means that there is hardly any chance in factor analysis of dividing those variables up into more or less homogeneous groups indicating dimensions of language competence. The probability of a one-factor-solution is rather high from the very beginning, without proving very much about the structure of the variables under investigation as it is (or might be) in reality.

We would consider it to be a clear piece of evidence for the assumption of one-dimensionality, therefore, only when a one-factor-solution shows up even if a large number and a broad variety of tests are included in analysis. Yet in cases like this the probability of the appearance of more than one factor rises again, as is demonstrated by studies in which twelve or even more language variables have been included (cf. Carroll, 1958; Pimsleur et al., 1962; Gardner and Lambert, 1965; Löfgren, 1969; Bonheim and Kreifelts et al., 1979; Scholz et al., 1980). In all of these studies statistical analysis led to at least three different group factors, but again, none of the structures found can be interpreted materially in terms of the strong form of the divisible competence hypothesis.

It should be added that in the majority of these cases one of the factors found (usually the first one) was often more "general" in nature, contributed to by a broad range of sub-tests in varying constellations (through *not* being the *only* component of test variance). This very finding has also led to the consideration of "weaker forms" of the UCH—although strictly speaking this may have looked like a logical contradiction in itself to many of us (cf. Oller's definition of the *Partial Divisibility Hypothesis* as follows: "there will be a large chunk of reliable variance shared by all of the tests, plus small amounts of reliable variance shared by only some of the tests" (1979:425). In my own understanding this position characterizes one of the many alternatives among the multi-dimensional models; it already marks the end of the UCH, of which no weaker form can exist.

Things have developed further in this direction. Even when a general factor in the original sense of the term appeared it was shown that this result was partly induced (or produced) by the specific method applied (especially principal components analysis with its disadvantage of not dividing up common variance from test-specific and error variance). Moreover, it was shown that different results could be obtained with different computational procedures and under fuller specification as to the causal relationships assumed.

In other words, a one-factor model can always be substituted for—at least in theory—by a number of other models with equal or better heuristic value, even when they are underidentified. Accordingly, a general factor can always be split into successively finer subfactors depending on the desired level of theorizing. This is one of the striking results of Upshur and Homburg (1980).

As to the methodological side of the issue it is generally agreed now that among the different methods used the principal components analysis seems to be particularly inadequate because it tends to overestimate the significance of the first factor (the main reason for this has just been given; cf. also Sang and Vollmer (1980), Vollmer (1980) or Vollmer and Sang (1983) for a detailed discussion of this problem). I would no longer go as far as to assert that a general factor thus appearing was artificially produced, a mere statistical artifact. But the results obtained from factor analytic investigations are definitely open to manipulation (Raatz, 1980). In some of our reanalyses mentioned earlier it was shown that the application of (common) factor analysis in contrast to principal components analysis could indeed change the factorial structure (cf. also Raatz (1980) who demonstrates in a systematic way how such manipulation can be carried out).

Using factoring methods in general in a purely *exploratory* manner (that is, not stating in advance what might be the outcome, hoping for a structure to appear which was not thought of before) seems to be highly unsatisfactory for the resolution of the issues at hand. Factor analysis in its classical form is a handy tool for reordering data and simplifying description, as we know, but it is not at all an objective method which can be used to examine the validity of a theory of the structure of language (cf. again Raatz, 1980). Therefore, *confirmatory* factor analysis, as already applied by Bachman and Palmer (1981) and Purcell (1983), is clearly to be preferred among all procedures. This statistical method is more powerful because the data gained are tested against a structural hypothesis which has to be stated explicitly beforehand. Other suitable methods would be path analysis (as used by Upshur and Homburg, 1980) or componential analysis (as developed by Sternberg, cf. for example, 1977 and 1980).

Recently, another method of factoring has been proposed which is otherwise less often used today, namely a principal components analysis carried out on the covariance matrices (cf. Hughes and Woods, 1982). Although the authors give some reasons for choosing this method, it is not at all clear in my opinion what the advantages and disadvantages of this form of analysis are or how powerful a method it is. Moreover, unless it is demonstrated how this procedure compares to the other factoring methods generally used, it will be extremely difficult in the future to make any meaningful comparisons with other research results.

Possibly we have been too much preoccupied with the assumption of factorial causality, with the interpretation of factors as underlying abilities or "latent traits" within an individual. This interpretation has been seriously questioned. Consequently, a critical reassessment of classical test theory as well as psychometric theory is under way. One of the main criticisms concerns the problem of rotation, whether or not to rotate factors at all and, if the decision to rotate is made, how to do so. Due to the fact that this can be done in an (almost) infinite number of ways and due to some other severe limitations of factor analysis some critics have gone as far as to question the meaningfulness of relating factors (as mathematical abstractions and chance products) to "traits" or abilities (as hypothetical psychological constructs) altogether (cf. for example, Mandl and Zimmermann (1976); see also Sternberg (1977 and 1980), offering the best summary, in my opinion).

Leaving this controversy as it is, I have my doubts that factor analysis will bring us much further at all at this particular point in development. Since we are having to ask ourselves what our tests really measure, we rely on validation studies other than those aiming at "convergent" validity. But this is only part of the answer. More specifically, we need research based on an information-processing approach (including experimental studies) that will help us to understand the psychological processes in comprehending and producing meaningful utterances in L2 better than we do now. For only when we grasp more deeply the cognitive potentials as well as the task-specific processes, strategies and operations which are involved in language learning and testing shall we be able to arrive at a clearer picture as to how these tests function and what the meaning of a correlation between any two of those tests is. It is only then that the application of factor analysis may be appropriate again under certain conditions.

Certainly, the need for a greater variety of theoretical models of foreign language competence, and for more powerful and diverse statistical methods is generally accepted now. Interestingly enough, the introduction and advancement of *hierarchical* models has not really overthrown the UCH as being wrong altogether. Rather, the notion of a general factor is revised only as to its claim of being exclusively appropriate in mirroring what competence is (or could be). As a matter of fact, a strong first factor (being either complex or even general in nature) *may* or *may not* continue to show up in future studies largely depending on the model employed and the computational procedure used—in any case it does not *mean* the same any more as it was supposed to during the past years (namely, an indication of a *unitary* competence or a global, indivisible language processing device). Yet all that the reinterpretation of the general factor has led to is the enlightened view that it is "componentially complex" (cf. Oller, 1983c) in the sense that it represents the highest level of abstraction within a comprehensive model of ordered levels of ability or, if you like, the deepest level of the hierarchy pervading it all.

Accordingly, competing hypotheses about second language ability are no longer thought to be mutually exclusive, but rather complementary. To put it in Oller's own terms:

> Formerly it was thought (by me if no one else), that dividing up the variance in a global factor was logically incompatible with the existence of such a factor. This incorrect premise led to the conclusion that models which pictured language proficiency as divisible were logically incompatible with holistic models (Oller and Hinofotis, 1980). That conclusion was incorrect, not because holistic models are not appropriate, nor because particulate or componential models are inappropriate, rather because *both* are appropriate. *Componential and holistic models are complementary, not mutually exclusive.*   (Oller, 1983c).

Certainly I agree with Oller on this point (as a matter of fact, Sang and I have speculated on this complementary relationship ever since 1978; cf. for example, Sang and Vollmer 1978:27–29). Yet it remains unclear how far this consensus goes. In the paper from which I have quoted Oller himself deals with two arguments against a general factor—the so-called "so what" and the "statistical-artifact" approaches. As to the latter he tries to prove that a general factor is "in fact a reflection of genuine language abilities" (Oller, 1983c)—using *abilities* in the plural. Shortly after, however, on the same page he speaks of his opinion that "in most practical contexts we are not interested in finely grained diagnosis but in overall capability". Are we still to assume then, that such an "overall capability" (as a basic abstract propositional reasoning capacity of mankind) psychologically really exists? Maybe Davies was right in labelling this a "philosophical question" that seemed to him "not amenable to proof" (cf. Davies, 1982).

The implications of a *componential approach* to the study of foreign language competence (based on information-processing theory) have only just begun to be investigated and understood in more detail by the research community. Therefore, I would like to correct myself and not speak of a general *shift in focus* (or change of paradigm) yet (cf. Vollmer, 1982). Although the information-processing approach apparently suffers from none of the intrinsic limitations of the factor analytic method, it certainly has its own weaknesses, too. As Sternberg (1977:63) remarks, none of the three methodologies (computer simulation, substraction method, additive-factor method) within the information-processing approach seems to "(1) provide a means for studying systematically correlates of individual differences in performance; (2) provide a common language across tasks and investigators; or (3) prevent overvaluation of task-specific components". In developing componential analysis, Sternberg wants to synthesize an approach "that would capitalize upon the strength of each approach, and thereby share the weaknesses of neither" (1977:65).

It remains to be seen how far this alternative procedure will lead us in solving some of the intricate problems in the analysis of human abilities in general and in the study of foreign language abilities in particular.

Perspectives

My outlook can be fairly brief because some future perspectives have already been touched upon. Let me add just a few more.

The relationship between basic cognitive operations and capabilities on the one hand and domain-specific cognitive processes on the other has to be studied further. How far can we assume *language-specific* cognitive structures or linguistic abilities to exist earlier than, next to, in competition with, independent from, or as part of *general* problem-solving abilities; what sort of evidence do we have for either one position (cf. Felix, 1981)?

What does the assumption of a specific language acquisition device

(LAD) for acquiring one's native language mean in terms of the structure and quality of language aptitude in general and foreign language aptitude in particular, defined as a "talent", a "readiness" or whatever? And how does Lenneberg's "latent biological structure" as well as Selinker's "latent psychological structure" relate to the concept of (foreign) language competence?

As to the relationship between L1 and L2 abilities the issue of language universals will have to be followed up. In addition, the specificness of the L2 acquisition (either in a natural or in a formal-instructional setting) will have to be elaborated upon. What constitute specific properties within a foreign or second language learner's competence (cf. Faerch and Kasper, 1980, or Vollmer, 1981b, for the notion of strategy and strategic competence; see also Sang (1983) and Vollmer (1980, 1983) for their empirical contributions in the analysis of the interaction between L1/L2 abilities)?

From a cognitive developmental (Piagetian) point of view the cognitive possibilities of a human being should be fully developed by the time of the onset of puberty when the final stage is normally reached with formal operations being available.

How does this obvious change in cognitive capacities effect the differences between first and second language acquisition and how does it relate in particular to the assumption of an adult L2 learner's diminished ability to acquire native-like command of the target language.

Generally speaking, the interlanguage hypothesis in its updated version (cf. Selinker and Lamendella, 1981) as well as contrastive models of second language acquisition will have to be worked upon and put to use for the issue at stake. In interlanguage modelling and theorizing, for example, a micro-behavioural, neurofunctional perspective is now being outlined.

Also, the empirical work of Soviet psychologists as well as that of Lompscher and his colleagues (GDR) on mental abilities (cf. for example, Lompscher 1972, 1976) seems well worth considering and incorporating into a theory of foreign language competence. Within this school of thought, a number of basic mental activities have been identified and defined in operational terms (such as ordering, class construction, classification, differentiation, generalization, abstraction, exemplification, induction, rule formation and application, understanding of the relationship between part(s) and the whole, relating properties to objects etc.).

In addition, another level of ability has been defined, referring to typical and habitualized qualities and peculiarities with which an individual structures his/her overall mental activity. A number of categories have been offered to describe these qualities (such as anticipation; facility, fluency, and speed of execution, degree of precision and quality, degree of activation and independence; planfulness or systematicity; flexibility; strategicness in concept formation or problem-solving processes; sensitivity, creativity, and the like—the German term would be "Verlaufsqualitäten der geistigen Tätigkeit").

Next to these rather stabilized (yet nevertheless acquired) structural components of cognition a third level of ability is postulated—that of situation-dependent and task-specific "actuality" in the mental actions of a learner including motivational and attitudinal aspects.

Finally, in the theoretical framework referred to here a very close relationship is seen between the development of knowledge and the quality thereof (being the software of mental operations) on one side and the unfolding of operational skills and abilities on the other, as outlined above.

Since foreign language abilities as viewed in this paper are neither innate nor fixed but are considered to be open for change, it will be very important to find out what change is mainly based upon (dissatisfaction, internal conflict and restructuring, training etc.). As the implicit knowledge of a foreign language grows the abilities to incorporate new items or rules into the existing structures or schemata and the abilities to apply this knowledge more or less appropriately in differing communicative contexts will also increase. We know very little about the dynamic and yet systematic character in the development of a foreign language learner's grammar as a whole, about "stages" or "infrasystems". The correctness of the fossilization hypothesis has in any case yet to be proved.

A number of controversial issues will also have to be followed up with more effort: it may be that the structure of foreign language competence is not the only source of individual differences—motivational and attitudinal factors such as willingness to learn or to use the language at all and proper chances to do so have been mentioned in the literature. In any (future) study these factors will have to be better controlled for.

Independent of the question of what (causal) model our data can best be explained by, one of the main deficiencies in research so far has been, generally speaking, the limited range of variables investigated (often only aiming at the receptive skills).

In order to arrive at a sounder judgement on the dimensionality of language ability one would always have to include a variety of tests to measure *productive* performances, namely tests of writing and speaking within different settings, catching important speech functions on the discoursal and communicative level. As a guideline, one should perhaps measure the four integrated skills by at least three different methods and instruments each (combining various approaches and formats). In addition, we will have to take the necessary precautions to ensure that our samples are more or less homogeneous as to the range of previous experience and exposure, because heterogeneity of a sample might very well lead to the appearance of an artificially strong first factor (without having a substantial meaning in terms of a structural hypothesis; cf. Raatz, 1980; or Hughes and Woods, 1982).

Moreover, one and the same individual may use different language varieties in different situations and it looks as if no systematic data will be possible until the characteristics of the situation are clearly defined, as Tarone (1979), among others, argues.

Finally, from a componential point of view, individuals may choose alternative paths in solving a language task (implying different sequences of steps, combinations thereof, different levels of consciousness, differing degrees of option or number of steps or different processes altogether. How could this be interpreted in terms of ability structure (learner-specific versus task-specific abilities, optional versus obligatory components, abilities actually used versus those required by task-specification)?

Componential analysis is likely to lead to a widening understanding of the nature and functioning of (foreign) language ability and subsequently to its redefinition in the long run. On the other hand, it may very well be that too many hopes are projected upon this approach which is not substantially developed as yet and in large parts still rather vague. In order to illustrate or assess its usefulness for foreign language testing somewhat further, I shall make a few more comments.

Basically a component is defined as a hypothetical process in the human mind.

> A component is an elementary information process that operates upon internal representations of objects or symbols . . . The component may translate a sensory input into a conceptual representation, transform one conceptual representation into another, or translate a conceptual representation into a motor output. Componential Analysis is therefore akin to information-processing analysis in that its elementary unit is a process rather than a construct representing a static source of individual differences.
> (Sternberg, 1977:65; see also Sternberg 1980:574)

In this theoretical and methodological context Sternberg classifies components by function as well as by level of generality. As to the first criterion, he considers components to perform (at least) five kinds of functions.

> *Metacomponents* are higher-order control processes used for executive planning and decision making in problem solving. *Performance components* are processes used in the execution of a problem-solving strategy. *Acquisition components* are processes used in learning new information. *Retention components* are processes used in retrieving previously stored knowledge. *Trans-*

fer components are processes used in generalization, that is, in carrying over knowledge from one task or task context to another.

(Sternberg, 1980:575)

As to the second criterion, three levels of generality are distinguished: a *general* component would be one which is "mandatory in all tasks of a specified kind", whereas a *group* or *class* component is optional. "It is used in only a subset (or group) of the tasks being considered" (1977:319). *Specific* components on the other hand are required to perform single tasks within the task universe.

Each component is said to have three important properties associated with it: *duration*, *difficulty* (error probability), and *probability of execution*. Methods and examples of estimating these properties of components have been described by Sternberg and others, although a certain preoccupation with the first one has been asserted (cf. J. B. Carroll, 1980:587). Components seem to be interrelated in a number of ways. More important yet, they are supposed to account causally at least for substantial parts of what is considered to be meaningful foreign language behaviour. This interpretation has been vigorously questioned, however, by Carroll (1980). For him, components are (merely) postulated mental processes, whereas factors are underlying sources of individual differences. He continues:

Technically a factor is a latent variable upon which each individual in a given sample on a given occasion has some specific value or "score". Any one or more of such factor scores may function as an independent variable, each with an appropriate weight or factor coefficient, in an equation for specifying the composition of a manifest, observed variable. One type of manifest variable could be a "component score." For example, the expected duration of an individual's encoding operation in an analogical reasoning task as estimated by the experimental and statistical procedures that Sternberg (1977) has outlined.

(J. B. Carroll, 1980:587)

According to Sternberg, on the other hand, factors should not be interpreted as "latent traits", but rather as mathematical representations of "reference abilities" defined as "constellations of components that in combination form stable patterns of individual differences across tasks" (Sternberg 1977:78).

There is no space here to go into any further details (the best critical account, however, of what the advantages and shortcomings of componential analysis might be is to be found in a recently published excellent overview article by Sternberg (1980) with open peer commentary and the author's response to it). One of the long range aims of componential analysis applied to foreign language testing, as I see it, would be to give several scores (instead of only one) to a learner solving a test item, one for each component or ability postulated or identified through intensive task analysis (in this context cf. the work of Stegelmann, 1980, for an extension of the Rasch model).

It is not totally clear to me whether componential analysis comprises factor analysis to a certain extent, or how far both approaches are to be viewed as complementing each other in the information they convey. As far as I can see there are a number of similarities, but also marked differences between the two procedures. One of them seems to convey information about individual differences in task or test performance (subject variance), the other one information about sources of differential task or test difficulty (task variance).

In addition, "factorial models tend to be structural ones, although they often contain clear implications for understanding information processing; componential models tend to be process ones, although they often contain clear implications for understanding how information is structured" (Sternberg, 1980:575). It is to be hoped that both the structural and the procedural approach will add to our knowledge of foreign language abilities, how they build up, how they function, in what way they are responsible for producing measured performance. This means finding out how knowledge of the rules (lists, networks, structures, schemata, etc.) interacts and increases (simultaneously?) with the facility and scope of mental operations in handling this knowledge more or less appropriately (filtering it, storing, retrieving, assembling, choosing, monitoring, etc.).

It remains to be seen how far factors can indeed be understood in terms of components on the basis of a comprehensive cognitive language learning theory.

This brings us to the final difference between factor and componential analysis: both procedures seem to serve somewhat different social purposes (such as predicting as opposed to diagnosing, explaining, and training performance). This also has to do with some macro-level of research in contrast to the micro-level of investigation. These are by no means alternatives in the sense that they are mutually exclusive, both types of research are needed, both are appropriate and compatible with each other. Both could highlight different aspects of our global and ill-defined concept of foreign language ability.

Remember that Oller, when trying to justify the appropriateness of the concept of a GLP within a hierarchical model of language competence, also pleaded for holistic approaches to testing once more. "It seems to me to make sense to do some componential differentiation in testing, but it also seems to make excellent sense to do some integrative testing as well. If I have to choose, I'll put most of my money on the latter" (Oller, 1983c).

In the long run, I would think, this decision is a matter of personal interest, of preference on some practical or social grounds, and, above all, of concentrating one's energy on either one or the other approach. Division of labour is asked for. Most likely, the alternative path via analytical experiments, finely tuned diagnostic testing and componential analysis is a stonier one, requiring more combined theoretical efforts by way of inter-disciplinary cooperation, and it will probably be some time before satisfactory results show up. But this complex task will have to be attempted by some of us at least.

Different researchers have begun to choose individual pathways to the study of (foreign) language ability and different levels of abstraction within a hierarchical model as their starting or focusing point—and will continue to do so. Some concentrate on what they consider to be the deep central ability (mentalese, the language of thought). Others have elaborated upon the distinction between comprehension and production in foreign language learning and communication in theoretical and operational terms (cf. Vollmer, 1981b). Still others have geared their research to the skill level or some particular skill, functional domain, or area of knowledge. Some have proposed or even started to experiment with miniature artificial languages (MAL) in order to isolate some relevant mental operations and processes which might also be involved in learning and using a natural foreign or second language (cf. McLaughlin, 1980).

Pragmatically, it makes sense to concentrate one's efforts on those parts or aspects of the issue where substantial results have shown up (e.g. specific skill areas) and continue from there on. On the other hand, however, with such divergent activities going on and different approaches being used, it will be ever more important to keep in mind the overall framework and theoretical questions from which these studies spring.

The research activities mentioned vary greatly as to the aspect, range, power, and appropriateness of their description and/or explanation. Concerning the third function of science, prediction, namely of a foreign language learner's mental activities in solving a language problem and (even more so) prediction of future success in using the L2 and communicating in it—it has become more difficult, I guess, for a number of reasons, some of which have been pointed to. I would consider it a misuse of any proficiency measurement(s), if powerful and long-range predictions, based on these test results, were made other than for narrowly defined situations in the near future which would have to be more or less systematically represented already in the item sample.

Testers will have to become leading theoreticians and at the same time stay good technicians in test construction and evaluation. I hope to have shown in this paper that it is actually *more theory* that is wanted and needed throughout. For only that which is being put into the construction of a particular test or set of tests by way of theoretical insight, reasoning, or hypothesis building *in advance* will come out of it substantially. It is a heavy burden and there is a long, long way to go.

2

Response to Vollmer

Where now?

Arthur Hughes

In the first paragraph of his paper Vollmer admits that, though we can now be sure that the Unitary Competence Hypothesis was mistaken, we are still a long way from discovering the true structure of foreign language ability. This is indeed the state of the art, and it is on the immediate implications of this for testing practice and for the conduct of future research that I wish to concentrate here.

If, as seems clear, there are separable components of foreign language ability, then it should be open to testers to measure learners' performance on each of them. Of course this is what testers already attempt to do when they construct batteries of tests with the intention of obtaining either some overall measure of language ability or more detailed diagnostic information. In the first case it may hardly matter what each of the sub-tests measures, whether in fact it taps an identifiable component of ability. It will hopefully still add to the reliability of the battery and, provided that there seems to be a reasonable spread of tasks, the test constructor will be satisfied that he is measuring something he can call overall language proficiency. If, on the other hand, the purpose of a battery is diagnostic, there is a problem. Certain components, it is true, have proved relatively easy to interpret with respect to test tasks. "Speaking ability" as measured by performance in an interview is an obvious example. Unfortunately, where analysis has concerned performance on tests related to linguistic levels or elements rather than integrated skills, the results have not been so clearcut. Scores on grammar tests, for instance, have not consistently revealed a grammar component when, along with other test scores, they have been subjected to principle components analysis or factor analysis. It is conceivable that this happens because what we would recognize as

DVLPMNTS IN LANGUAGE TESTING
ISBN: 0-12-360880-5

grammatical ability simply cannot be separated out from total skills. But this seems unlikely to me. We know of learners whose control of grammar lags far behind a rapidly expanding vocabulary (Zoila, in Shapira, 1978, and Blanca, in Hughes, 1979, being cases in point). It is probable that the particular samples of learners used in recent studies have contributed to the non-emergence of a consistent grammar (or vocabulary) component. But there is another reason, too. The tests used in these studies, though called 'grammar' tests, may not in fact measure what they are supposed to measure, as Oller amongst others has already suggested.

The way to determine whether we can identify a component of foreign language ability which we would all agree was grammatical must, in my view, be through the analysis of carefully elicited speech and writing, rather than of test scores. Doubts that might be held about the feasibility of doing this successfully derive from studies that show that judges appear unable to distinguish reliably between an individual's grammatical and his lexical ability (e.g. Yorozuya and Oller, 1980). The solution to this would seem to be for each judge to concentrate on only one element (e.g. grammar) of the speech or writing, and for there to be a sufficient number of judges assigned to each element for reliable results to be achieved. Given a reasonably narrow range of ability (so that differences *between* learners would not obscure differences *within* learners) and a large enough sample of output from each, it should be possible to isolate a grammatical and a lexical component. Once we can identify these we will be in a much better position to validate grammar and vocabulary tests. It would also be a useful first step in the direction of the more distant goals that Vollmer would set for us.

What Vollmer seeks is a theory of first, second, and foreign language ability which is sufficiently detailed to account for individual differences in processing and output, and which can be integrated into a more general theory of cognition. To achieve this he suggests the need to incorporate insights from a variety of sources (interlanguage studies, etc.) as well as the possibility of adding componential analysis to research techniques already used in the field. I am sure that such a theory, supported by research, is necessary for a full understanding of foreign language ability. But while we should keep this long-term goal in mind, I wonder if we are yet in a position to construct such a theory, except in the very broadest outline. Perhaps we would be better advised to content ourselves with research that may prove practically useful in the short-term and will provide information which will contribute to longer-term theory building. I shall develop this thought in the remainder of my response.

Vollmer welcomes a shift "from the macro-level of mathematical data reduction to a psychologically more informed and better motivated information processing view of language performance". Certainly, an account of how language is processed is essential to a complete understanding of language ability. It would also enable us to create new and more delicate tests in a controlled and principled fashion. While Vollmer accepts that each researcher must go his own way, he spends some time in extolling the advantages of componential analysis, directing our attention to the work of Sternberg (1977, 1980) in particular. I hope that he is right in thinking that this is a profitable line to pursue, but I have my doubts. In the first place, I am not convinced that we have a model of language processing detailed enough to test in this fashion. Secondly, I wonder if the language tasks on which performance would be susceptible to componential analysis could be anything but very trivial. Sternberg has been concerned with the study of analytical reasoning, which can be broken down into tasks which lend themselves to this kind of analysis. I shall be very interested to follow Vollmer's progress, but I suspect that for the time being more traditional methods of analysis carried out on carefully elicited data (including longer stretches of speech and writing) will prove more rewarding and of greater direct practical benefit to the testing community.

I will turn now to a consideration of the subjects whose language performance is to be analysed in future studies. Vollmer reminds us that a number of variables may contribute to similarities and differences between learners in their output and, presumably, the processes that underlie it. He mentions motivation, attitude, aptitude, and the influence of the learner's first language. Hughes and Woods (this volume) discovered differences in the structure of the performance on the Cambridge Proficiency Examination of four groups of students (from Norway, Mexico, North Africa, and Hong Kong). However, they were unable even to attempt to explain these differences because they simply did not know enough about their subjects. As Vollmer says, we really need to control for learner variables. This will not only help us to interpret the results we obtain, but may also allow us to make more meaningful comparisons between studies, something which Vollmer observes has been difficult in the past.

The fact that individuals can apparently differ quite considerably in the way that their foreign language ability is structured may make us wonder whether we are right to search for *the* structure of foreign language ability. It is true that some differences may be very superficial: speaking performance may be affected by shyness, for example. And no doubt there are features which all speakers have in common, which are inevitable in human beings. But given the complexity and plasticity of our brain, and the widely varying circumstances in which languages are learned, there may be considerable and significant differences in the way we actually process second or foreign languages. This is hardly a novel idea. It is just such a difference that was thought to distinguish coordinate from compound bilingualism. Just what these differences will turn out to be, and how significant they are, is of course a matter for research. In the meantime, however, testers must not forget that there *are* differences between individuals and between groups in the way that their foreign language ability is structured. We should be wary of generalizing from one group of learners to another, possibly quite dissimilar, group.

In the recent past there has been a remarkable convergence of interest among psycholinguists and language testers. For this happy state of affairs to continue, research must have some bearing on practical testing problems. Vollmer ends his paper by saying that testers will have to become leading theoreticians. Fine! But let them remain testers too.

3

Response to Vollmer

"g", what is it?

John W. Oller, Jr.

It is a pleasure to be able to comment on the paper contributed to this volume by Helmut Vollmer. There are many points now of substantial agreement. In fact, to prolong the discussion (an undesirable goal in any event) it would be necessary to bring an old battle horse out of a recent grave. In certain respects, Vollmer's discussion has done just that— presumably for the purpose of getting in a few last sound thwacks before we put the old beast back in its permanent resting place. However, we may agree at the outset that the objective is not so much to retire the theory in question, nor yet to reform it through drubbing, but to bury it. The idea of an exhaustive global factor of language proficiency was wrong.

As a result, the topic of "general" language proficiency may seem to have become what the topic of "general" intelligence became decades earlier—a topic out of fashion. Davies (as cited by Vollmer) apparently sought to declare it so. He called it a "non-issue". Still, the topic lingers. It is difficult to declare an issue dead when the very act of declaration revives the issue and in effect places it on the agenda for further discussion. So, the topic of "g" still haunts us. We wonder, "What is it?"

Obviously, it isn't everything. That is, it is not a unitary and exhaustive factor encompassing all the variance generated by tests that engage language abilities. On the other hand, the arguments that "g" is just a statistical artefact, or an illusory mirage of maturation, seem less than fully persuasive. If there were no "general" language factor associated with "knowing a language natively" or with "communicative competence" then why would it make any sense to speak of such things as if they had some kind of coherence, unity even, or at least integrity? Or, putting it differently, isn't it possible that some type of "general" factor will be *necessary*

DVLPMNTS IN LANGUAGE TESTING
ISBN: 0-12-360880-5

to a theory of language proficiency? Or to a theory of the capacities underlying language use?

I still think that "g" is a useful, even a necessary construct. However, the holistic, global aspects of language use, or other cognitive performances, do not exclude particulate, analytic and discrete elements. Indeed, it seems that in an adequate theory the holistic aspects must depend on the interaction of relatively analytic components. Hence, the idea that global and particulate models were incompatible must have been quite wrong from the outset (e.g. see Oller and Hinofotis, 1980). It would seem that both views are needed and that they can complement each other rather than contradict one another. It seems to me that the argument of Upshur and Homburg (forthcoming) showing that any "g" factor will necessarily be decomposable into contributing components in many different ways, is very persuasive. On the other hand, I would be inclined to suppose that the numerous components that go to make up language capacity (the general sort) must fit together in some sense even before they are integrated and manifested through the process that we loosely refer to as "language acquisition". That is to say, not only is some sort of global factor dependent for its existence on the differentiated components that comprise it, but in their turn, the components are meaningfully differentiated only in relation to the larger purpose(s) to which all of them in some integrated (integrative?) fashion contribute.

Of course, the foregoing paragraph cannot be construed as anything more than the mere glimmerings of a theoretical perspective. Somewhat more detail (but not very much more) can be found in Oller (1981, 1982). A major point of agreement with Vollmer is that we need to concentrate much of our energy in the future on working out better theoretical models. The disagreements will probably relate to just what portions of previous theories should be included or excluded in the formulation of the new models.

In this regard, there are three points which are brought up by Vollmer where we seem to differ. First, and most important, the concept of "expectancy" as an element of language proficiency has not been abandoned. The reasons for postulating this construct are unchanged. It is true that Neisser weakened his own position, but that change, in my view (see comments on Vollmer and Sang, forthcoming), did little or nothing to undermine the claims for the temporal development of ordinary experience and language use. In this connection, see Oller (1983b) for a non-technical update on the "expectancy hypothesis", and related topics. In brief, it seems clear to me that one of the functions of grammatical systems is to generate expectancies concerning the classes of elements that are likely to appear next in a string—whether the elements are phonological segments, morphemes, phrases, clauses, or larger units of discourse.

Second, I do not agree that the models examined by Bachman and Palmer (1981) were "half-hearted" or lacking "in any meaningful theoretical perspective" (Vollmer, this volume: 8). In fact, I agree with Vollmer's remarks elsewhere suggesting to the contrary that their work is exemplary of the sort of hypothesis testing that is sorely needed. No doubt other and better models will eventually be tested, but this is no reason to deny the existence of sound theoretical reasoning underlying the important work that Bachman and Palmer have contributed.

Third, though I agree with Vollmer that factoring methods will have be supplemented by clearer models and more developed theoretical reasoning, I do not think that we should lightly dismiss factor analyses even of the exploratory type. While it may be salutory that much of the enthusiasm for factoring methods has been dampened by recent developments, the tools of simple correlation, exploratory factoring, multiple regression, and analysis of variance, should not, I think, be cast aside entirely. Neither should we expect more of confirmatory methods than they can provide. It would seem that what they offer in hypothesis-testing muscle, they compensate for by exacting a high toll in prior assumptions—many of which remain largely untestable.

In fine, then, I am happy to join Vollmer in shovelling a bit of ceremonial dirt into the hole where the old UCH now lies buried. At the same time, it is also gratifying to be able to agree with him that the theoretical problems which accompanied that hypothesis have survived the debacle. We must still, it seems, deal with the question of just what any given general factor represents, as well as the question of what components go to make it up. In fact, aren't these questions, at base, the same? If this is so, then perhaps as Vollmer himself has suggested, we have indeed returned to stand on territory staked off by Robert Lado and others who were here before us.

4

Fourteen years on—later thoughts on overall language proficiency

Bernard Spolsky

In a paper unusually refreshing for its confession of error, Oller (1980) says that he was wrong in his claims for the strong version of the unitary factor hypothesis, which held that there was a single factor in language proficiency which could even turn out to be the same central factor that accounts for general intelligence. On the second part of this claim, he is now much more cautious than ever before:

> With the state of theory being what it is, it may in fact be premature to try to judge too dogmatically whether deep language ability and intelligence are really distinct. (1980:134)

On the unitary hypothesis itself, he says that his earlier position has been proved wrong, and blames his error on an unfortunate use of the principal components analysis, a statistical technique which

> inflates the estimated general factor significantly and tends to depress the appearance of any other specific or group factor. (1980:134)

In his paper, Oller attributes the idea of the unitary factor to researchers "who expected to be able to find a large 'central' factor of language proficiency"; he cites in particular Spolsky (1973 and even earlier) and Upshur (1969). Intrigued by this association with the birth of a now-discredited heresy, I have been attempting to reconstruct the arguments that I first put forward some 14 years ago. As often happens, the chronology is complicated by delays in publication. Spolsky (1973) was written some years earlier, forming a cluster with two papers written and presented in 1967: Spolsky (1967) presented at the NAFSA Conference and published in the same year, and Spolsky *et al.* (1968) read at the Michigan

DVLPMNTS IN LANGUAGE TESTING
ISBN: 0-12-360880-5

testing conference and published in its proceedings: and with the summa-
tive theoretical paper written to be presented at the 1969 AILA Congress
(Spolsky, 1971).

In these papers, I saw the notion of overall language proficiency as more
or less equivalent to, and by acknowledgement derived from, John Carroll's idea of integrative language tests. I quote a section from the NAFSA
paper which makes this connection clear:

> The high correlation obtained between the various sections of TOEFL and
> other general tests of English suggests that in fact we might be dealing with a
> single factor, English proficiency. . . The unreliability of . . . a measure of
> overall proficiency led to emphasis on the development of discrete point
> tests.   (1967:38)

In the Michigan conference, the acknowledgement to Carroll is made:

> Fundamental to the preparation of valid tests of language proficiency is a
> theoretical question: What does it mean to know a language? There are two
> ways in which this question might be answered. One is to follow what Carroll
> (1961) has referred to as the integrative approach and to say that there is such
> a factor as overall proficiency.   (Spolsky et al., 1968)

The two main arguments presented for this approach are empirical and
theoretical. The empirical argument followed from the work of a number of
scholars including Holtzman (1967) who were at the time reporting high correlations between various language profiency measures; the papers published by Oller and others at UCLA in the early 1970s produced continued
support for this notion, until the statistical fallacy was pointed out. My
second argument was theoretical: it focussed attention on the link between
the creative aspects of language knowledge and the ability to operate in
conditions of reduced redundancy provided by the work of Miller and Isard
(1963) and others. I saw this as giving support from information theory for
such tests as dictation with or without added noise and the cloze technique
which made use of the principle of reduction of redundancy.

While hindsight always helps, one recognizes a number of hedges and
some caution in the original presentation. For instance, due allowance was
made for the effect of the test method itself: the NAFSA paper pointed out
that the "lack of perfect correlation between the various parts (of TOEFL
and other general tests) could possibly be a distortion of the measure"
(1967), an interpretation supported by the recent studies of Bachman and
Palmer. Further, there was no suggestion that overall language proficiency
tests were all that were needed: there was recognition of the value of
discrete point tests in diagnostic testing:

The discrete point approach obviously has much value in deciding whether a given feature has been mastered, and in doing so it controls a teaching process. (1967:39)

One area of fuzziness seems to have taken me a while to work out, and that was the communicative aspect of language use. I quote from the Michigan conference paper:

> We are using the overall approach when we attempt to give a subjective evaluation of a foreign speaker of our language. In such cases, we usually do not refer to specific strengths and weaknesses, but rather to his overall ability to function in a given situation. We do not say, "he is unable to distinguish between /i/ and /iy/" but rather something like, "He can't follow lectures". (1968a:79)

How this functional ability relates to overall proficiency is left vague in the pre-1970 papers, but discussed in detail in a paper I wrote with three graduate students in 1971:

> . . . levels of knowing a language cannot be characterized in specific linguistic terms, that is, as mastery of a criterion percentage of items in a grammar and lexicon. Proficiency tests must be based on a functional definition of levels. Tests are needed not of how many items a subject may know (although of course this is a reasonable question in an achievement or diagnostic test) but of his ability to operate in a specified sociolinguistic situation with ease or effect . . . (1972:222)

Tests like the FSI Oral Interview which fits this definition are complex and expensive to administer, but one solution is to develop overall proficiency tests that make use of the principle of the reduction of redundancy. Another solution, illustrated in detail in the rest of the paper, is to develop functional tests of communication.

There are also, I am pleased to discover, early adumbrations of my more recent concern with the ethics of language testing (see Spolsky, 1981). The NAFSA paper spent some time considering the irrelevance and possible danger of using a language test score as a criterion for university admission; a paper read at the 1968 TESOL convention made reference to "degree of doubt" in the interpretation of tests results, and the "functional" paper was quite blunt:

> Results (of these tests) are gross, classifying rather than ranking students but this is appropriate to the goals. And there is likelihood of a certain amount of error, but this is not disguised by complex statistics . . . (1971:231)

What I do miss in these earlier papers, and wish I had managed to express, was a realization that any individual's overall language proficiency might be made up of very different functional abilities. The high correlations that show up over groups of subjects disguise the enormous potential for individual variation. I suspect that for all my caution, I was still hoping for a single and simple solution to what I now would accept as an unresolvable problem. For the principle of uncertainty has at last found its way into language testing. As Oller puts it,

> The hope of simplicity . . . has been lost. . . . If we examine language proficiency from the point of view of communicative effect, it has a kind of holistic quality that cannot be denied. On the other hand, if we begin to try to understand what is meant by communicative effect and how this holistic quality is achieved, we find ourselves on a road with many junctions.
>
> (1980:142)

On such tension, our world too must rest.

Note

This paper was written for presentation at the BAAL Seminar on Research in Language Testing, my attendance at which was supported in part by the British Council and in part by Bar-Ilan University.

5

Principal components and factor analysis in the investigation of the structure of language proficiency

Anthony Woods

Introduction

Vollmer has already documented in this volume the attempts of many authors to analyse the scores of groups of subjects over a number of language tests to determine the inherent dimensionality of such data.

They hoped to discover whether the important features of the structure of such data sets could be expressed by means of a single variable, a "general language factor". If it were not so, they hoped they might be able to identify, in terms of linguistic concepts, what components or factors, other than the general ability factor, might be involved in "language competence".

Two widely used techniques for the reduction of multivariate data sets to sets of smaller dimension are Principal Components Analysis (PCA) and Factor Analysis (FA). Most specialist texts on Multivariate Analysis, for example Kendall (1980), Morrison (1976), Marriott (1974), Maxwell (1977), Bennett and Bowers (1976), make a clear distinction between the mathematics and motivations of the two techniques. However, in a recent book on Multivariate Methods in Human Communication Research (1980), Hunter presents PCS as a special case of FA, and a number of personal communications received by this author in response to a paper, Hughes and Woods (1981) in which PCA was carried out on language testing data, make it clear that the difference between the two approaches is still not well understood. This lack of understanding is likely to promote their inappropriate application or hinder their effective use in research into the nature of language competence.

DVLPMNTS IN LANGUAGE TESTING
ISBN: 0-12-360880-5

The essential difference is that PCA is a descriptive technique which simply presents a different view of the data without making any assumptions, while FA requires the assumption of an explicit model superimposed on the data by the investigator. It is true that a PCA can be used as a first step in one particular method for solving the mathematical problems posed by FA and this is the most likely cause of the confusion between the two techniques. However, a detailed discussion of both types of analyses makes it clear how different they really are.

Principal components analysis

Suppose a number of subjects are each tested by means of p different tests of language ability. The score for each subject can be written as a vector $(x_1, x_2, \ldots, x_p)$, where x_i is his score on the i-th test. A component is a simple linear combination of the p test scores. For each test we must identify a coefficient by which we multiply the corresponding test score. The weighted scores are then summed to give a single value. In this way, the set of test scores for a given subject can be converted into a set of component scores for that subject, each component being defined by its own set of weights or coefficients. A unique set of components, the *principal components*, can be obtained by introducing a few simple constraints.

The first component is defined in such a way that the scores of the subjects on this component will have as large a variance as possible. In a sense we may say that the first principal component accounts for as much as possible of the total "scatter" or variation in the complete set of test scores of all the subjects. Further components are then chosen successively to be uncorrelated with all previous components and to have as large a variance as possible. This process will continue until there are as many[1] components as tests and at that point the total variance of the (uncorrelated) components will equal the total variance of the (correlated) test scores.

We should recognize, however, that the variability in the test scores comes from two sources. The first is the difference in the ability of the candidates to perform the tests. The second is the random measurement error in each test due to the way in which a given subject's score would vary over different instances of the same test. PCA makes no attempt to partition the variability into the proportions relevant to these distinct sources, and the variance of each component will have contributions from both. On the other hand, PCA does not require any assumptions about the statistical distributions of the test scores nor of the scores of the subjects on any latent constructs comprising the different dimensions involved in the concept of language competence. PCA involves only a reorganization of the observed test scores into uncorrelated components, which are each a weighted sum of the original scores and which are ranked by their variance in decreasing order.

There is no model behind PCA. Indeed, principal components are obtained by rotating the original coordinate system for the data, defined in terms of the test scores, until the new axes lie along the directions of greatest variability. The new coordinates in such a rotated system will always be *exact* linear combinations of the old coordinates, so that, *of necessity*, the principal components are weighted sums of the test scores.

Consider the simple case of two test scores, x_1 and x_2, observed for a large number of subjects. Each subject can be represented by a point plotted on the (x_1, x_2) axes corresponding to his scores in the two tests. If the set of points is cigar-shaped, that is noticeably elliptical, the first principal component will correspond to the direction of the long axis of the ellipse. If this ellipse is very narrow, the score of a subject on this first component will contain almost all the information in the pair of test scores and it ought to be possible to devise a single test with the same power to discriminate between subjects as the pair of tests taken together. If, on the other hand, the scattergram of the test scores is nearly circular, then two components will always be necessary and we may as well stay with the original tests.

It should be apparent from this that the results of a PCA are scale dependent, since the shape of the data plot can be altered dramatically by altering the units in which we measure one or more of the test scores. Carrying out a PCA on the correlation matrix of the test scores is equivalent to scaling each score to have mean of zero and variance of one, and it is possible that the principal components based on the correlation matrix may be quite different from those extracted from the covariance matrix of the original scores, as is confirmed by Hughes and Woods (1981) and Kendall (1980:Tables 2.4 and 2.6). Thus, if a PCA is being considered a decision has to be taken whether or not to standardize the test scores.

If the variables to be analysed in a PCA are measured in reasonably commensurable units, i.e. they are all lengths or weights or exam marks, as is the case with different language tests, then a weighted sum of those variables, such as a principal component, is a quite natural object and it is a legitimate statistical exercise to maximize the variance of such a component. This suggests that PCA should be carried out on the covariance matrix of the raw, unstandardized test scores. After all, we wish to choose the first principal component to explain, as far as possible, the variances of the test scores and it seems artificial to make all those variances equal, before analysis, by standardizing the scores. Morrison (1976:268) states that "maximization of such total variance of standard scores has a rather artificial quality" although he comments that "most applications of the technique (PCA) have involved the correlation matrix, *as if in keeping with the usage of factor analysts*" (my italics). Anderson (1963) has shown that the sampling theory of components extracted from correlation matrices is exceedingly more complex than that of components based on analysis of a covariance matrix. All authors seem to agree that, if it is felt sensible to carry out a PCA on variables which are not commensurable, e.g. age, income and IQ score, then it will be necessary to standardize the variables and use the correlation matrix. However, as suggested above, where the variables are commensurable, such as language test scores, it seems more natural to use the original test scores with the variances and relative weights established naturally by the performance of the subjects and by the range of scores possible on each test.

As stated earlier, there will be as many principal components as original variables. In general, many of these will have a very small variance and we may feel that the first few, possibly just the first, can explain a sufficient portion of the variability. However, it is not only the relative variance of a component which determines its importance, but rather the extent to which it describes a residual feature of the data set after the earlier components have been extracted. Eastment and Krzanowski (1982) have proposed an iterative test for choosing the minimum number of components required to explain the structure of the data set. Their method makes no assumptions about the statistical distribution of the test scores and is a type of "least squares" technique related to the methods of linear regression. The principal components are considered one by one in order of decreasing variance until a decision can be made that all those components have been extracted which correspond to special features of the data. The decision is based on whether the addition of the next component introduces more noise than information into the description of the data offered by the previous components. Hughes and Woods (1981) describe the analysis of data from the Cambridge Proficiency Examination using the Eastment and Krzanowski criterion. The analysis was carried out for a number of sets of subjects each from a different examination centre and in every case the need for more than one component was clearly indicated.

Factor analysis

Suppose as before that we have p test scores for each of a large number of subjects. To carry out a Factor Analysis on the data we have to assume that they will be a reasonable fit to a model with the following features.

1. There are m, uncorrelated, underlying constructs or dimensions cal-

led factors (m<p) which can explain all the *correlations* between the test scores.

2. If a subject's "true" score for a given test could be obtained without measurement error, then it would be exactly a weighted sum of his true factor scores. The weights are usually called the loadings of the factors for that test score. These loadings are assumed to have the same value for all subjects.

3. The true test scores for a subject cannot be known because of random measurement error and hence no test score is an exact linear combination of factor scores. There is always random error known usually as the specific variance of the test.

4. The specific errors for different tests are uncorrelated with one another and with the factors.

5. It is usually assumed that the true scores for each factor over the population of subjects follow a normal distribution. This implies that the test scores are likewise normally distributed.

We see that in FA we make special allowance for the measurement errors. Moreover it is easily shown that the relative values of the factor loadings for any test are independent of the units in which the test score is measured. These are two points in favour of FA.

However, while in PCA it is a fairly easy task to compute the weight to be given to each test score in its contribution to each component, it is quite a different matter to determine the loadings in an FA. This is largely because we do not know the factor scores of the different subjects. All we have is the assumption that these scores are normally distributed. Neither do we know the specific variances of the tests.

In fact, the problem is indeterminate. The factor model cannot be solved unless further mathematical restrictions are imposed. There are several perfectly legitimate ways of doing this and some technical discussion of the problem can be found in Horst (1963). Each of these methods will lead to a different solution. Even then, each solution is only one of a possible family of solutions for a given number, m, of factors. Each method will lead to the determination of a coordinate system with m axes in which, according to the model, the original test scores can be represented exactly, except for measurement error, and each axis corresponds to a different factor. If the axes are rotated while remaining mutually at right angles, any rotation will also be a solution to the original problem. Every rotation will, of course, change the values of the favour loadings and hence the interpretation of the factors.

A related difficulty with the interpretation of either FA or PCA is that samples chosen from the same population can give rise to factors or components which look quite different from one sample to another. Such sampling variation is not unusual, it is met in ordinary tests of hypothesis or in the estimation of means or proportions, but, in PCA, or FA, its effects are poorly understood and difficult to allow for.

However, to decide for or against the UCH, we need only consider, to begin with, the *number* of underlying constructs required to explain the test scores. Can we decide how many factors are required, assuming the factor model to be valid? Again, we must realize that sampling variation can cause under or over estimation of the number of factors.

Various criteria have been suggested. One due to Guttman (1954) suggests that a factor should be included only if it accounts for at least as much of the variance as any of the test scores. It can be shown (see any of the texts mentioned earlier) that a possible measure of the "explanatory power" of a factor is the sum of the squared loadings on that factor. Factor Analysis is generally carried out on the correlation matrix which means that each test score has been standardised to have variance equal to one. Hence we might include only those factors whose sum of squared loadings has a value greater than one. (A mathematician would say that the eigen value of the correlation matrix associated with such a factor has a value greater than one.)

Another, equally *ad hoc*, criterion, suggested by Bennett and Bowers (1976), is that to be considered important a factor should account for at least 10 per cent of the total variance.

However, if the factor model really is considered to be valid, there is a respectable statistical criterion available. First a number of factors is chosen. Using maximum likelihood methods it is possible to estimate all the parameters of the model, the loadings and specific variances, *conditional on the number of factors*. A statistical test can be carried out on the null hypothesis that the chosen number of factors is sufficient to explain the structure of the data. If the hypothesis is rejected, it is assumed that more factors are required. An example of such an analysis is given in Kendall (1980, Chapter 4), and it seems that seven factors are required to explain his data set containing fifteen variables. The last three of these factors have associated eigen values much less than unity, and *together* they account for only 11 per cent of the total variance! The maximum likelihood method of fitting the factor model has not been widely used in the past because the calculations involved require a large and powerful computer. Recent versions of SPSS do include this option for implementation on suitable machines. Bachman and Palmer (1981) do use maximum likelihood in a confirmatory factor analysis to test that a particular factor model can be supported by data.

Of course, as with all tests of hypotheses, a significant value of the test statistic can have many causes. Suppose we obtain a value which suggests we should reject the hypothesis that two factors are sufficient to explain a set of test scores. This may have occurred because

1. two factors are not sufficient, though the factor model would fit with a higher number of factors;
2. two factors are sufficient but do not bear a linear relationship to the test scores, for example each test score might be a weighted *product* of the factors;
3. the factor scores, and hence the test scores, may not have a normal distribution;
4. measurement errors may be correlated (e.g. because of interviewer bias in spoken language tests) and so cause spurious factors to appear; Maxwell (1977:57);
5. the model may fail in some other way—Rao (1965) believes the factor model is always unrealistic;
6. the model is correct, two factors are sufficient and the significant value is simply due to sampling error.

It is possible to check the data for some of these deficiencies and certainly if one could obtain reasonably compatible results from a series of analyses on several sets of independent data it may be possible to have some confidence in the conclusions. In general, though, grounds can usually be discovered for doubting the soundness of inferences based on the factor model, and extreme care is required in the interpretation of data through Factor Analysis.

Principal components or factors?

There are two questions one ought to ask at this stage: is it likely that the Unitary Competence Hypothesis can be proved or disproved by means of the kinds of multivariate methods discussed above, and, if it can, which of the two techniques is likely to be most relevant? It may help to summarize the important features of PCA and FA and compare them.

PCA attempts to explain, with as few dimensions as possible, the scatter of the test scores over subjects, that is to explain or, rather, describe succinctly how the profiles of test scores differ between subjects. It has been used traditionally for classification of subjects, particularly by numerical taxonomists in biological classification. FA on the other hand looks for a small number of constructs to explain the correlations between test scores, that is, to explain the degree to which different tests measure the same thing. Since the two techniques have different purposes they may very well give quite different results. They are measuring different effects, neither of which may coincide with what we mean by linguistic ability.

PCA uses no model, it allows the data to tell its own story. However, this lack of a hypothetical model is likely to favour the occurrence of a general component, a kind of weighted average of the scores, which accounts for a very large proportion of the total scatter of the data. This artefact is well known to taxonomists who have tended to describe this first component as the "size" component and discard it as uninteresting! (Penrose (1953) discusses the size effect.) It seems that the test of Eastment and Krzanowski may frequently indicate the need to include later components even when the first principal component accounts for a rather large proportion of the total variance.

Factor analysis, on the other hand, requires the assumption of a highly structured model. This alone makes it more likely that more factors than principal components will be indicated by the same data. This is similar to the difference in results expected from parametric and non-parametric tests in the univariate case. If the model is correct the parametric test will be more sensitive, more powerful. If the model is unjustified then it is likely that such tests will give spuriously significant results.

PCA does not separate out measurement error from between subject variability, while FA does. If the factor model is correct, this may make factors easier to interpret and, in any case, one has the option to rotate the axes of the factor solution to look for factors with a simple interpretation. However, there may arise through rotation several interpretable sets of factors and it will be difficult to choose between them.

For both PCA and FA, the degree of homogeneity of the group of subjects is important. In an early paper on FA, Spearman (1904) complains about researchers attempting to make their subjects as diverse as possible rather than as alike as possible. We might consider the problem, for example, of trying to discover what determines "athletic ability". If we choose our sample from the complete population of adults, it is likely that a general measure of physical fitness will have overwhelming importance. If we choose a sample of athletes then we may find that we can group them sensibly into runners, jumpers, vaulters, swimmers and throwers.

No researcher dealing with a single variable or test score would lump together into a single sample subjects who were expected, on *a priori* grounds, to belong to distinct populations. Nor would he distort any samples he might choose by weighting them heavily in favour of the extremes. Yet this is done *deliberately* by Yorozuya and Oller (1980), who choose a sample of only ten foreign students such that "they ranged from the lowest level to the highest proficiency level represented at the institute. This selection was intended to produce a maximum range of proficiencies among the interviews to insure optimum variance in scores across interview." Apart from the fact that this procedure ignores the above mentioned warning of Spearman against too great a heterogeneity in the group, it clearly rejects the basic experimental precaution of choosing *random* samples.

So can the UCH be resolved by using Factor Analysis or Principal Components Analysis? There are some indications that the weight of evidence is against the hypothesis. Although some authors, e.g. Oller and Hinofotis (1980), believe they have identified a single component or factor (the words appear to be used interchangeably!) which is sufficient to account for all the important relationships in a set of test scores, the force of such studies is gravely weakened by the failure to choose the subjects in an acceptable fashion and to adopt an objective criterion for a decision about the number of components required to explain the structure of the data. Certainly when reasonably homogeneous groups have been used, as in Hughes and Woods (1981), it has been possible to find, using the Eastment and Krzanowski criterion, that several components were required, though sometimes they were rather difficult to interpret. Vollmer points out that he has usually managed to detect more latent dimensions in the data with FA rather than PCA, but it is not clear what criteria he has used to choose the required number of components or factors; what is more, he seems to have carried out the PCA on the correlation matrix, and there is always the question whether the factor model is justified.

Furthermore, in the end we must not lose sight of the most important reason why such analyses can never prove the correctness of the UCH. Even if it could be agreed what is meant by a reasonably homogeneous group and that the factor model was justified and if it transpired that repeated PCA and FA could discover only a single dimension in the data, these results would refer only to sets of test scores. That is, the current tests measure only one dimension of language competence. Would linguists be sufficiently confident in their knowledge of this concept to be certain that there did not exist a dimension which fails to be tested by all the current language tests?

In summary, PCA analysis using the Eastment and Krzanowski criterion has demonstrated that the Unitary Competence Hypothesis is not tenable, in that data sets consisting of the scores of a substantial number of students over several tests cannot be explained adequately by the first principal component. I believe that this is as far as we can go at present in *testing* hypotheses about the nature and dimensionality of language competence through the multivariate analysis of test scores by means of Principal Components Analysis or Factor Analysis.

However, PCA and FA, properly used on suitable data sets, can be excellent devices for exploratory analysis of language test results to suggest hypotheses and to look for ways of reducing the number and complexity of language tests.

Note

1. It is possible to construct data sets which will give rise to fewer components than variables. In practice this rarely happens unless the number of variables is greater than the number of subjects or unless one or more of the scores is a linear combination of some others, for example when the total score for each subject is included as an extra variable.

6

Interpreting the performance on the Cambridge Proficiency Examination of students of different language backgrounds

Arthur Hughes and Anthony Woods

Introduction

This paper investigates the performance on the Cambridge Proficiency Examination (CPE) in June 1980 of 324 subjects representing four linguistic-geographic groups: Norway (108), Mexico (93), North Africa (53) and Hong Kong (70). A short description of the 19 sub-tests that make up the CPE is given in the Appendix, p.61; the means, standard deviations and ranges, together with the correlation coefficients between scores on each sub-test and total scores on the examination, are to be found in Table 6.1.

Principal Components Analysis (PCA) was carried out on the variance–covariance matrix (rather than on the correlation matrix) for the reasons given in Woods' paper in this volume. The Eastment and Krzanowski (1982) procedure was then used to determine the number of components needed to account for the data. The results for each group were as follows:

Norway: 4 components (accounting for 51%, 15%, 6% and 6% of the variance)
Mexico: 3 components (49%, 14%, 10%)
North Africa: 2 components (61%, 13%)
Hong Kong: 3 components (67%, 7%, 6%)

This work was carried out originally in response to Oller's support of the

DVLPMNTS IN LANGUAGE TESTING
ISBN: 0-12-360880-5

indivisibility (or unitary competence) hypothesis. One expression of this hypothesis (Oller, 1979:425) includes the claim that the indivisibility hypothesis allows *only* for a general component of test variance. Once such a component is accounted for, the indivisibility hypothesis predicts that any residual variance will be due entirely to random variation none of which can be reliably attributed to real differences in the performance of the subjects in the various tests. The evidence of our CPE study contradicts the hypothesis expressed in that form and Oller himself has rejected it (see his paper in this volume). More than one component is needed for each group; this much is certain and has already been reported (Hughes and Woods, 1981). What we shall do in this paper is to look more closely at these components to see whether their structure allows their plausible interpretation as the expression of recognizably "real" abilities.

Structure of the principal components

We begin by examining the correlations of the first five components for each group with each of the 19 sub-tests (Table 6·2; only correlations of 0·25 or over are given). We notice immediately that in every case the first component has a reasonable correlation with all the sub-tests, and that the correlations have the same sign. It might be thought that this is an indication that for each group there is a "general" component. Certainly it indicates that, over each complete group, any sub-test score is a more or less good linear predictor of total examination score. It must be remembered, however, that each candidate can be expected to have prepared for the examination and to have had practice on all of the sub-tests. Clearly this would tend to make their performance over all the sub-tests more uniform than it would otherwise have been; thus the "general" component may be in part the outcome of rather specialized training.

Furthermore, it has to be noted that it is entirely usual that a PCA should give rise to a first component that is a simple weighted average of the variables included in the analysis, especially when the subjects studied have a wide range of ability. Reducing the ability range will reduce the importance of this "general" component and may cause it to disappear entirely. In this study we carried out PCA on three groups each of 34 of the original subjects, of various nationalities, consecutively ranked according to their total examination score. One group was chosen from the upper end of the range, one from the middle and the third from the lower end. The results are given in Table 6·3.

It is immediately apparent that no general component can be identified. This is not surprising. A general component of the type which appeared previously with each of the four original groups is simply a weighted average of the scores on the various sub-tests and as such is a measure of the subjects' overall ability. By restricting the range of the total scores we have constructed groups within which the subjects are of very similar abilities overall, and their scores on any "general" component would likewise be similar. As a result, any such component would account for very little of the variance between subjects within these homogeneous groups and would have little importance. Hence no such component appears in the PCA. If the unitary competence hypothesis were true, no components at all would be indicated by a PCA carried out in these circumstances, but that does not happen. The differential performance of individuals on the various sub-tests is sufficiently non-random to give rise to significant components even in the absence of notable differences in their general level of ability.

What have we learned so far? That, given a wide range of ability, performance on one language task is generally a reasonable predictor of performance on another, especially where the subjects have been trained for those tasks. This is quite unremarkable. Our knowledge of the way skills are transferred in other fields would lead us to expect it. What it does not tell us, most decidely, is anything about the processes underlying performance of the various tasks. It would be odd, we may admit, if there were no shared processes or stores in the various language tasks. Be this as it may, the emergence of a general component throws no light on the nature of these processes. In other fields, such as biological taxonomy, researchers discard the first component as unilluminating. We can do the same.

Comparison of the four groups

When we turn to the other components it seems possible to make sense of at least some of them. There does appear to be a speaking component for both Hong Kong (Component 3) and North Africa (Component 4, though this is not significant); while Mexico (Components 4 and 5) and Norway (Component 5) have components where speaking ability plays an important part. It might be thought that such a "speaking" component is an artefact of the way we have subdivided the tests to give six speaking sub-tests, or of the method of analysis. There are strong indications that this is not the case. We computed the scores of individuals on this component and looked more closely at individuals scoring very high (2 SD above the mean) or very low (2 SD below the mean). In the case of the Hong Kong speaking component there are four such cases. These subjects have similar overall scores, but they perform very differently on the speaking tasks (sub-tests 8–13):

	Total Score	Speakers' Sub-test Scores
Subject A	106	878646 (39)
Subject B	131	988888 (49)
Subject C	127	332203 (13)
Subject D	123	223331 (14)

We have here subjects whose speaking ability is either well above or well below their ability on the other examination tasks. Since we have identified them by means of their scores on the component, this suggests that the component is, in this case at least, real enough.

North Africa Component 2 and Hong Kong Component 2 are very similar (and Mexico Component 3 is not very different). There is a contrast here between vocabulary knowledge (as measured by the multiple choice test) and the ability to read rather long passages of English and answer open-ended questions on them. The opposing signs in the component (plus as against minus) simply mean that scores on this component will be positively correlated with one sub-test (say vocabulary) and negatively correlated with the other(s). In other words, this kind of component accounts for the variability in subjects' performance which comes about by a subject performing rather well on some sub-tests and rather poorly on others. We may note that Hong Kong Component 4 concerns ability to respond to a rather *literary* passage. Norway Component 2 relates to all *writing* tasks with the addition of cloze. And Norway Component 3 contrasts the sub-tests involved in Component 2.

If finally we turn our attention to Mexico Component 2, we find that there are 14 outliers, 12 scoring very low on the component, two scoring very high. What is immediately striking is the number of non-Hispanic (and non-Indian) names, at least 5 of the 14. In particular there are two subjects with English names whose total marks were above average (180,208) but who performed poorly on sub-test 7 (which is correlated 0·83 with the component). It seems likely that these two subjects are native speakers of (or bilingual in) English. It also seems likely that they had not prepared thoroughly for the kind of task that the sub-test provides them with, questions about "irony", "extended metaphor", etc. It is specialized training that they lack. This ability does not follow from being a fluent speaker and writer of the language. We are reminded that degree and quality of training is an unmeasured and uncontrolled variable in this study and in others with which we are familiar.

Conclusion

We have shown that more than one component is needed for every group to account for performance on the Cambridge Proficiency Examination. We have interpreted some components and shown that they may be real. This would indicate that no single "global" test will be accurate in its prediction of the ability of individuals (as opposed to groups) to perform the kinds of tasks, such as the speaking sub-tests, associated with these components. If we want to measure an ability accurately, then as far as possible we have to measure *it*, and not what we think may underlie all language ability. What we have not done, except in relation to the two subjects with English names, is attempt to *explain* differing abilities on the components, or the similarities and differences between the linguistic/geographic groups. We may think that differences of national character and differences of training, as well as innate human qualities, have played a part. We may think that a full explanation will require knowledge of the processes of language production and reception. We shall only be able to attempt such explanations when we have careful experiments with well known, or at least well controlled, variables.

Table 6·1. Means, standard deviations, ranges and correlations with total score

Sub-test	Norway		Mexico		N. Africa		Hong Kong		All		r with total
	$\bar{x}$	SD	$\bar{x}$	SD	$\bar{x}$	SD	$\bar{x}$	SD	$\bar{x}$	SD	
1 Multiple choice Vocab	24·2	8·1	22·5	5·9	19·6	7·1	23·0	6·7	22·5	7·2	·73
2 Multiple choice Read	7·0	1·2	7·1	1·4	5·8	1·8	5·2	1·6	6·4	1·6	·62
3 Multiple choice Read	8·0	1·8	7·8	1·6	5·8	2·3	6·0	2·1	7·2	2·1	·73
4 Multiple choice Listen	11·8	2·3	11·5	2·2	9·1	3·2	9·1	3·1	10·7	2·9	·77
5 Essay (describe/narrate)	11·4	2·6	10·8	2·0	7·1	2·4	8·3	2·6	9·9	2·9	·77
6 Essay (discuss)	10·6	2·6	10·1	2·1	6·9	2·4	7·8	2·4	9·2	2·8	·75
7 Extended reading	9·9	4·1	10·9	4·9	7·9	5·0	6·4	5·2	9·1	5·0	·66
8 Conversational communication	7·5	1·1	7·2	1·4	5·6	1·5	5·1	2·0	6·6	1·8	·73
9 Conversational vocabulary	7·2	1·3	6·8	1·4	5·1	1·6	5·1	1·9	6·3	1·8	·74
10 Topic communication	7·5	1·4	6·9	1·5	5·3	1·5	5·3	2·1	6·5	1·9	·75
11 Topic grammar	7·1	1·5	6·7	1·5	4·8	1·6	5·2	2·1	6·2	1·9	·78
12 Pronunciation	7·4	1·5	6·5	1·6	5·0	1·3	4·7	2·0	6·2	1·9	·75
13 Situations	7·4	1·2	6·6	1·8	6·2	2·0	4·7	2·0	6·4	2·0	·68
14 Cloze	14·4	3·2	13·0	3·2	10·4	4·5	8·6	4·3	12·1	4·3	·87
15 Paraphrase	8·3	2·4	8·1	2·6	6·4	3·0	5·1	2·7	7·2	2·9	·74
16 Completion	9·1	2·1	7·1	2·3	5·4	2·8	4·4	2·5	6·9	3·0	·77
17 Paraphrase	7·2	2·1	6·2	2·3	6·1	2·8	4·3	3·3	6·1	2·8	·73
18 Summarize	17·6	3·9	17·1	4·7	14·2	5·5	13·1	5·8	15·9	5·2	·79
19 Style	5·3	2·5	4·8	2·0	3·5	2·5	1·8	2·4	4·1	2·7	·64
Complete test	188·9	29·1	177·6	29·9	140·2	40·0	132·2	44·0	165·4	42·1	
Total range	117–255		114–265		51–220		51–255				

Table 6·2. Correlation coefficients of components with sub-tests (only coefficients of over 0·25 shown)

Sub-test	1	2	3	4	5	6	7	8	9	10	11	12	13	14	15	16	17	18	19	T	V%	
Norway																						
1	·95	·43	·50	·58	·46	·44	·33	·35	·36	·42	·45	·37	·36	·59	·50	·50	·47	·64	·42	·89	51	X
2					·42	·45	·74							·48				·35	·35	·40	15	X
3					·44	·41	·30							−·30				−·56		·00	6	X
4								·32		·30			·30			·36				·16	6	X
5					·35	−·44	−·47	·52	·55	·57	·50	·49	·33						−·45	−·07	4	O
Mexico																						
1	·90	·25	·57	·46	·58	·63	·54	·50	·56	·51	·61	·54	·52	·79	·58	·63	·73	·73	·52	·98	49	X
2					·31		−·83													·02	14	X
3	−·36																	·61		·04	10	X
4				−·31				−·39	−·34	−·41	−·41	−·32	−·45		−·44	−·33				−·18	5	O
5								·53	·43	·51	·43	·42	−·33							−·03	4	O
North Africa																						
1	·90	·59	·82	·82	·69	·62	·62	·58	·61	·56	·66	·53	·51	·90	·63	·76	·59	·85	·56	·99	61	X
2	·38						−·72											−·37		−·04	13	X
3					·34	·43									·49		·35			−·09	5	O
4								·62	·58	·67	·48	·48	·45							·07	4	O
5												·30				−·40	−·32			·07	4	O
Hong Kong																						
1	·91	·51	·68	·80	·77	·76	·86	·59	·61	·69	·71	·69	·58	·87	·78	·72	·84	·85	·45	·99	67	X
2	·32						−·25											−·43		−·01	7	X
3																				−·16	6	X
4							−·41	·67	·68	·64	·59	·52	·51							·00	4	O
5																			·62	−·02	3	O

X = significant, O = non-significant; figures under V% indicate percentage variance accounted for by each component.

Table 6·3. Coefficients of principal components for reduced range groups (only coefficients of 0·20 or over are shown).

Comp't		SIG	V%	1	2	3	4	5	6	7	8	9	10	11	12	13	14	15	16	17	18	19
Upper	1	X	27%	0·53						−0·66											−0·44	
	2	X	17%	−0·67				0·24		−0·38	0·20	0·21					−0·22			−0·21		
	3	X	15%							−0·50						−0·21					0·65	0·27
	4	X	11%					−0·62	−0·46	−0·28										0·28		
Middle	1	X	29%	0·66						−0·70											−0·24	
	2	X	25%	−0·62						−0·62											−0·68	−0·35
	3	O	9%	0·27			0·26	−0·66									−0·26		0·30			
	4	O	8%				0·33		−0·31								0·30		0·30			
Lower	1	X	30%	−0·80						0·22	0·21						−0·21				−0·29	
	2	X	22%	0·21						−0·56											−0·69	
	3	O	10%	−0·42				−0·26		−0·62							0·22	0·22	0·27		0·33	
	4	O	9%							0·34						−0·26	0·52	0·45		0·36	−0·38	

X = significant, O = non-significant; figures under V% indicate percentage variance accounted for by each component.

Appendix 6·1

The 19 Sub-tests

A sample examination, with a teacher's book, is published as "Certificate of Proficiency in English, Testpack 1" by Cambridge University Press, and is available from booksellers. What follows is intended to give the reader only some idea of the various sub-tests used in this study.

1. Multiple-choice vocabulary (40 items); supply missing word in single-sentence context.
2,3. Multiple-choice reading comprehension (each 10 items); questions on passages of about 600 words in length.
4. Multiple-choice listening comprehension (15 items); 5 questions on each of three passages read twice.
5,6. Essays; one requires the student to describe or narrate, the other to discuss.
7. Extended reading; the candidate answers questions of a rather literary nature (e.g. what is the extended metaphor . . .) on a passage of English. Scoring is without reference to the quality of expression shown in the answers.
8. In a conversation based on a photograph the candidate is scored for overall communication.
9. In the same conversation the candidate is scored for vocabulary.
10. The candidate speaks on a prepared topic for about two minutes. He is scored for overall communication.
11. He is also scored for "grammar and structure" for his performance on the prepared topic.
12. The candidate reads one part in a dialogue, the examiner the other. Scoring is for pronunciation.

   8–12 are all scored on a ten-point scale.

13. Situations. The candidate responds verbally to three situations put to him by the examiner. Scoring is out of three for each situation.
14. Cloze (20 items); rational deletion and acceptable response scoring.
15. Paraphrase (10 items); the first word or two of the paraphrase is given.
16. Sentence completion (8 items); mid-point of sentence omitted, the candidate having to fill the gaps "with a suitable word or phrase".
17. Paraphrase (9 items); with the requirement a given lexical item be used in making the paraphrase.
18. Summarize (14 questions); candidates answer questions on passage of about 750 words, a test of their ability to "understand, interpret and summarize".

19.   Style. The candidate is required to convey information in a particular form or style.

7

The effect of quantity of context on the ability to make linguistic predictions: a flaw in a measure of general proficiency

Don Porter

Introduction

It is part of the rationale for cloze tests that a reader—or for that matter a listener—draws on the sum of his knowledge of a language, in interaction with his knowledge of the world, in the continuous generation of expectancies concerning what is about to be said, on the basis of what has been said. This process is also retrospective: the reader/listener continuously checks his expectancies against what actually *is* said, and also confirms or rejects his original interpretations in the light of subsequent utterance. The cloze test is thus considered to be a means of assessing the ability to use the various discourse constraints ranging over a text in order to set up and then confirm or modify linguistic predictions; this ability is widely held to be a characterizing component of general proficiency in a language.

We know from simple linguistic analysis that these constraints may be wide-ranging or local. It is a matter of considerable interest, however, to know whether in making predictions the listener or reader makes use of the full range of constraints, or whether he is primarily dependent on the immediate context. If the latter is the case, this could be taken as implying either that relatively small amounts of language are processed at a time in listening and reading, or that there is more than one level of processing going on, only one of which is concerned with linguistic prediction and checking, while other, quite different levels are concerned with more general, more wide-ranging strategies of comprehension.

There would also be implications for cloze procedure itself. If the reader

DVLPMNTS IN LANGUAGE TESTING
ISBN: 0-12-360880-5

or listener uses only local information to make predictions, it is unnecessary—though perhaps still convenient, to present cloze items in continuous text. Moreover, it would be difficult to argue on theoretical grounds for cloze procedure as an integrative technique for measuring general proficiency, proficiency in reading or listening, or even the global comprehension of a particular written or spoken text.

Research in this area has mainly taken the form of investigation into the effect of varying amounts of linguistic context on the predictability of items. Burton and Licklider (1955) found that while predictability of the following letter increased as knowledge of the foregoing text was extended from zero to approximately 32 letters in English texts, increasing the number of known letters beyond 32 did not result in any further notable rise in predictability, implying that the more distant constraints of style, syntax, subject matter, etc. were comparatively unimportant as clues aiding prediction: redundancy, of letters at least, appeared to be primarily important at local level.

However, the ability to predict the next letter would presumably depend primarily on the ability to predict the word in which it occurred (and also, of course, on ability to spell), Aborn, Rubenstein and Sterling (1959) accordingly considered the relationship between quantity of context and predictability of single words in various positions in isolated sentences. Although they found a consistent increase in the predictability of words in 11-word sentences over words in 6-word sentences, they found no appreciable difference in predictability of words between 11- and 25-word sentences. This finding tended to support Burton and Licklider's conclusion that redundancy does not on the whole increase in step with increasing quantities of context, once a certain minimum of context is supplied.

The fact that Aborn et al.'s experiment was concerned with randomly chosen, isolated sentences led MacGinitie (1961) to raise the question of whether the constraints upon individual words in continuous text might be cumulative, extending over longer sequences than single sentences. Using whole paragraph texts of 144 words each, he tried a number of deletion-patterns in which n (number of words between deletions) ranged between 2 and 23. He found that increasing n beyond 5 words to 11 or 23 did not help in the restoration of the missing words. This was, however, perhaps not surprising as the quantity of context from which the reader may derive clues to help him predict is not delimited by the two deletions on either side of the word to be replaced, but will always be the whole passage, diminished only by the number of unreplaced deletions. Thus if every 24th word were deleted from one of MacGinitie's passages, over 95 per cent would remain available as context to each deletion. If the deletion-rate were quadrupled to every 6th word, over 83 per cent of the passage would still remain.

Salzinger, Portnoy and Feldman (1962) drew similar conclusions to MacGinitie's on finding that, in a series of specially constructed 50-word passages at varying orders of statistical approximation to English, that one group of subjects showed no greater ability to predict deleted words with 6 words on either side (i.e. deletion rate every 7th) than a second group showed with 4 words on either side (deletion rate every 5th). These writers too concluded that subjects either do not or cannot make use of a context of more than 5 words on either side of a deletion. Once again, the conclusion is mistaken in that deletion-rate does not dramatically affect the true quantity of context, which is not bound by the deletions on either side. In this case, moreover, the conclusion is also rather shaky in that it is based on evidence from a very few deletions, in passages which are only approximations to English, comparing only two deletion rates, and those not strikingly distinct.

Fillenbaum, Jones and Rapoport (1963) found a moderate increase in scores as deletion rate was decreased from every second word to every 3rd, 4th, 5th and finally 6th word in a transcript of free speech. This is comparable to Burton and Licklider's finding that predictability of letters increases with preceding context up to 32 letters (= approx. 5 or 6 words), and Aborn et al.'s finding that words in 11-word sentences were more predictable than words in 6-word sentences (i.e. average bilateral contexts of 5 and 2½ words respectively). It is moreover consistent with the view that the whole of the remaining passage constitutes available context: at these high deletion rates slight decreases in rate produce major increases in quantity of context: a change from every 2nd to every 3rd word means an increase in available context of 1/3, while a further change to every 4th word means a further increase of 12·5 per cent. As the deletions become less frequent, so the gains in available context become smaller and the additional information assisting prediction becomes less significant.

Finally in this brief review of literature suggesting that quantity of context is *not* an important factor in the predictability of linguistic items, Alderson (1979a and b) also draws the conclusion from investigations of the effects of varying deletion rates that: "Increasing the amount of context on either side of a cloze gap beyond 5 words has no effect on the ease with which that gap will be clozed" (1979b:117). I can only repeat that the context in a cloze test will be in fact much greater than 5 words.

Evidence pointing in the opposite direction, supporting a quantity of context effect, is claimed by Oller and colleagues. Oller (1975) reports an experiment in which five prose passages were successively cut into 5, 10, 25 and 50-word segments, the segments then being presented in scrambled order. He found that for native speakers deleted words in the 5-word segments were significantly more difficult to replace than the same words deleted in the 10-word segments, and so on, and concluded that "cloze

items are sensitive to constraints that range beyond the previously estimated limits of 5 to 10 words on either side of a blank".

Nevertheless, Chihara, *et al.* (1977) considered that the cut-and-
scramble procedure used in the above study might have biased the results
through not taking account of sentence boundaries. These writers therefore carried out an experiment similar to that of Oller (1975), but in which
the scrambled units were whole sentences, and the comparison was made
with performance on the same sentences in sequential prose. Once again,
items in the scrambled sentences were shown to be significantly more
difficult than the same items in the original sequence.

Oller (1979:360) considers MacGinitie's (1961:128) objection that
"scrambling the order of the segments probably not only obscures the
paragraph topic . . . but also reduces restoration scores through misdirec-
tion and confusion", but takes these remarks as confirmation that cloze
items are indeed sensitive to larger contexts. Oller thus does not feel that
the validity of his own "scrambling" experiments is called into question. It
is *not* immediately obvious, however, simply because a link can be shown
to exist between an increasing incidence of linguistic confusion and a
decreasing predictability of words, that the predictability of words will
therefore improve with increasing amounts of non-confusing context. Chihara *et al.*'s claim (1977:64) with respect to Oller (1975) that: ". . . it has
been demonstrated that greater amounts of surrounding contexts increase
the ease with which subjects supply missing words . . ." is simply not
justified.

Because of the importance of the implications of any quantity of context
effect for our understanding of the reading/listening process, and because I
felt that the issue had *not* been successfully resolved so far, the following
investigation was undertaken.

Investigation I

Materials

Ninety-six segments of authentic text were selected from newspapers,
books, letters, written ephemera, radio and TV broadcasts, recorded
speeches, conversations, etc. These segments were randomly selected,
except in that they had the following characteristics:

1. Twelve were eleven words long, to give a blank plus a bilateral
   context of 5 words; a further 12 were 13 words long to give a blank
   plus a bilateral context of 6 words, and so on up to 12 segments
   consisting of a blank with a bilateral context of 12 words. Thus a test
   was produced consisting of 12 segments of text at each of 8 bilateral

context quantities ranging from 5 to 12 words. The segments were presented in random order. Subjects were asked to write into each blank the single word which made best sense.

2. Half of each set of 12 segments were taken from spoken language, and half from written.
3. Cutting across the spoken-written distinction, half the segments were derived from formal and half from informal language.
4. Finally, and equally distributed across the other variables, one third of the segments were chosen to begin at the beginning of a sentence (Initial Segments), one third began 5 words from the beginning of an utterance (Medial Segments) and one third ended at the end of a sentence (Final Segments).

Once the segments had been thus selected, the deleted words were assigned to their individual word-classes and also classed overall as "content words" (adjectives, nouns, lexical verbs and adverbs) or "non-content words". Each segment was analysed for syntactic complexity and assigned an index according to a formula developed by Botel, Dawkins and Granowski (1973).

The variables to be taken into account in investigating the effect of context quantity were thus *medium, formality, sentence-position, word-class* and *syntactic complexity*.

Subjects

The test was given to 3 groups of 50 subjects each, mostly students and staff (academic and non-academic) at the University of Reading. Group A was composed of 50 native speakers who were told to take as long as they liked over the test. Group B was composed of 50 native speakers under pressure: they were told to do the test as quickly as possible, but in any case not to take more than thirty minutes. Group C were non-native speakers, and were allowed to take as long as they liked. Subjects were grouped in this way in the hope that information might be gleaned on whether it is the most or the least proficient who make most use of the wider context in processing text.

Procedure

Subjects were allowed to take the test away with them. Those in group B were trusted to adhere to the time limit; in fact some people in group A completed the test in well under 30 minutes.

In accordance with time-honoured tradition, the test was scored in two ways—firstly by taking only the exact word deleted as correct, and secondly by taking any word as correct which was both syntactically and semantically acceptable. A word was deemed acceptable if it was given by a minimum of 10 people in the native-speaker group. The predictability of a deleted word was thus taken to be indicated by the number of subjects able to replace that word correctly, and the general predictability of words at a particular context quantity was taken to be the mean number of subjects successfully predicting words at that quantity.

Results

Considering each of the three groups of subjects in turn, scored by each scoring method, for each individual variable and for each combination of variables (a total of 684 separate sets of figures) there was no evidence anywhere of a gradual increase in predictability of words as the quantity of context increased. It would clearly be impractical to present the whole of this data here; we shall therefore let the global figures speak for all (Table 7·1). Simple inspection is sufficient to show the lack of a gradual context quantity effect. In fact, predictability varied considerably from context quantity to context quantity, and from item to item, suggesting strongly that factors other than context quantity were having a greater effect on subjects' ability to predict—if indeed quantity of context was having any effect at all.

There remained the possibility that bilateral increments in context of a single word at a time were too slight to have much effect, and that clear increases in frequency of prediction would be seen where the increment was markedly greater. In order to explore this possibility with the data available, the lowest three context quantities (5, 6 and 7 words bilateral) were combined and compared with the total of the uppermost three context quantities (10, 11 and 12 words bilateral) for the mean number of subjects successfully predicting each item. If increased quantity were to have any effect on predictability, we would expect the means for the uppermost quantities to exceed those for the lowest quantities. The number and percentage of the variables and variable combinations in which this was actually the case is given in Table 7.2.

It will be seen that with exact word scoring there appeared to be some tendency for items in the longer contexts to be more frequently predicted than items in the shorter contexts (approximately two thirds of the cases considered in each group). However, this was true only for exact word scoring, and even here the higher frequencies tended to exceed the lower ones by very small amounts (t values were not significant at ·05 level). Evidence such as this could be interpreted in favour of a context quantity effect on predictability only with the gravest of hesitations.

Table 7·1. *Subjects replacing words successfully: means and standard deviations. N (subjects) = 50; n (words at each context quantity) = 12*

Words bilat'l context	Group A Mean	SD	Group B Mean	SD	Group C Mean	SD
	Exact word scoring					
5	22·42	(18·54)	24·33	(19·68)	15·33	(16·77)
6	27·42	(15·29)	27·17	(16·05)	23·00	(17·47)
7	19·25	(19·04)	17·25	(18·19)	9·67	(14·07)
8	24·92	(15·73)	27·08	(15·61)	21·42	(15·04)
9	24·83	(18·15)	26·17	(18·59)	20·67	(17·81)
10	22·67	(17·04)	24·67	(17·41)	17·00	(17·01)
11	23·75	(19·75)	24·42	(19·73)	17·58	(16·72)
12	28·83	(11·84)	30·92	(11·72)	22·17	(12·01)
	Acceptable word scoring					
5	34·50	(9·45)	34·83	(11·48)	22·17	(14·96)
6	39·76	(7·34)	40·16	(7·84)	34·42	(12·95)
7	31·17	(14·78)	29·25	(16·23)	17·50	(15·25)
8	32·92	(10·93)	33·58	(12·15)	27·83	(12·34)
9	31·58	(13·11)	33·75	(11·72)	25·65	(15·81)
10	30·59	(13·13)	31·83	(14·06)	21·58	(14·87)
11	31·00	(14·09)	30·08	(16·37)	20·83	(15·00)
12	35·00	(4·82)	36·92	(4·98)	26·25	(8·76)

Table 7·2. *Number and percentage of variables/variable combinations for which mean frequency of prediction (high context-quantity) exceeded mean frequency of prediction (low context quantity). Total number of variables/variable combinations considered in each case = 114*

	Group A	Group B	Group C
Exact word	72 (63·16%)	76 (66·67%)	76 (66·67%)
Acceptable word	36 (31·58%)	44 (38·60%)	51 (44·74%)

If I may be permitted to step aside from matters of context quantity for a moment, I would like to comment briefly on the predictability of words with respect to the individual variables. Firstly, as one would expect, content words (adjectives, nouns, lexical verbs and adverbs) were regularly much less predictable than non-content words; they were more than twice as difficult to predict exactly for native speakers and almost four times as difficult to predict exactly for non-natives (Table 7·3). Secondly, there was little difference in the predictability of items derived from written and from spoken texts, though this may have been because the latter were presented in written form (Table 7·4). Thirdly, all groups predicted words slightly better in informal contexts (Table 7·5), though this was clearer in native speakers with exact-word scoring (p<·05).

Table 7·3. Subjects successfully replacing content and non-content words: means and standard deviations. n (content word) = 45, (non-content word) = 51

	Group A Content	Non-content	Group B Content	Non-content	Group C Content	Non-content
Exact:						
Mean	14·04	33·27	14·33	34·88	7·47	27·96
SD	(14·15)	(13·28)	(14·19)	(13·21)	(9·25)	(14·35)
Acceptable:						
Mean	26·02	39·75	25·56	41·06	14·24	32·86
SD	(10·54)	(7·64)	(11·84)	(7·36)	(10·10)	(11·48)

Fourthly, differences in the predictability of words in Initial, Medial and Final segments (Table 7·6) were in no case significant at the ·05 level. Fifthly, the two native speaker groups performed in very similar manner, the time pressure imposed on group B having no observable effect: perhaps the limitation to thirty minutes was too generous. On the other hand, native speaker scores on every variable were greater than those for non-natives, as one would expect; once again we can allow one set of figures to stand for all (Table 7·1). Sixthly, there appeared to be a very slight indication of a decrease in predictability with an increase in syntactic complexity indices (Table 7·7), but the difference in mean predictability between items in the syntactically least complex third of all the segments and those in the syntactically most complex third in no case reached significance at the ·05 level. Even if the measure of syntactic complexity used in this study is a reasonable one, therefore, the evidence presented here shows no obvious relation between the syntactic complexity of a segment and the predictability of a word in it.

Table 7·4. Subjects successfully replacing words in contexts derived from spoken and written language: means and standard deviations. n (spoken words) = 48, n (written words) = 48

	Group A Spoken	Written	Group B Spoken	Written	Group C Spoken	Written
Exact:						
Mean	25·15	23·38	25·71	24·79	18·63	18·08
SD	16·45	17·06	16·89	17·41	16·53	15·48
Accept:						
Mean	33·29	33·33	33·10	34·48	23·75	24·52
SD	11·21	11·68	12·28	12·63	14·71	13·92

Table 7·5. Subjects successfully replacing words in formal and informal contexts: means and standard deviations. n (formal words) = 48, n (informal words) = 48

	Group A Formal	Informal	Group B Formal	Informal	Group C Formal	Informal
Exact:						
Mean	21·06	27·46	22·10	28·40	15·69	21·02
SD	17·31	15·58	17·76	15·91	16·42	15·12
Accept:						
Mean	32·69	33·74	32·23	35·35	22·79	25·48
SD	12·19	10·61	13·49	11·15	14·61	13·96

Table 7·6. Subjects successfully replacing words in initial, medial and final segments: means and standard deviations. n (words in I, M or F segments) = 32

	Group A I	M	F	Group B I	M	F	Group C I	M	F
Exact:									
Mean	26·22	22·97	23·59	26·72	24·34	24·69	19·13	19·75	16·19
SD	16·85	15·75	17·77	16·84	6·09	18·63	15·52	16·28	16·25
Accept:									
Mean	35·88	31·19	32·88	35·66	31·91	33·81	25·16	26·13	21·13
SD	9·89	13·22	10·63	10·99	14·66	11·37	13·78	15·41	13·52

Table 7·7. Subjects successfully replacing words in 31 segments with lowest syntactic complexity and 31 segments with highest syntactic complexity: means and standard deviations

	Lowest complexity	Highest complexity
Exact:		
Group A: Mean	24·97	22·26
SD	16·59	16·86
Group B: Mean	25·06	25·23
SD	17·19	16·74
Group C: Mean	17·68	15·81
SD	14·79	15·33
Accept:		
Group A: Mean	36·03	31·10
SD	8·89	11·63
Group B: Mean	36·45	31·65
SD	9·99	11·95
Group C: Mean	24·48	21·39
SD	13·29	12·87

Finally, the pattern of results was generally the same for all three groups, in that what the non-native speaker found difficult, the native speaker was also less successful in predicting.

In spite of the scant evidence for a context quantity effect produced by this initial study, it might still be felt that the differences in context quantity dealt with were too slight for us to expect any great effect on the predictability of words in those contexts, and that a clearer increase in predictability might be expected when the quantity of bilateral context was increased dramatically. A follow-up investigation was therefore undertaken to explore this possibility.

Investigation II

Materials

A set of materials was obtained similar to those used in the first investigation, in that half were formal, half informal; within each of these categories half were derived from speech and half from written language, half were "content" words and half "non-content", and again each category consisted of one-third Initial segments, one-third Medial segments and one-third Final segments. Sequences were not graded for syntactic complexity, as this was a time-consuming operation which had been no more productive for the investigation than any other variable category, and had tended to relate to context quantity, making it difficult to achieve a proper balance of items with a particular syntactic complexity index at each context quantity. As before, sequences were selected randomly, and were composed of single blanks set in contexts at what was felt to be very different quantities: 5 or 6 words bilaterally, 11 or 12 words bilaterally, and 19 or 20 words bilaterally. There were 24 sequences at each quantity, making 72 sequences in all.

Subjects

The resulting test was administered to a single group of 50 native speakers, consisting of academic and other staff at the University of Reading, together with a few postgraduate students.

Procedure

Subjects were given as long as they wanted to complete the task of restoring deleted words. Some rushed through the task in little more than five minutes, while others spent a considerable time on it.

As there had been no question at all of a context quantity effect with acceptable word scoring in the first study, this test was scored for exact word restoration only. Predictability was again assessed in terms of the mean number of subjects successfully predicting words in the subcategory in question.

Results

Considering each of the individual variables in turn, and then a variety of variable-combinations, a total of 52 measures of predictability were considered.

Taking all types of context together, there was no ranking of predictability from high to low context quantity, nor was there such a ranking on any single variable. Of the 52 measures taken, only 5 ranked in the same way as the context quantity, and none of these showed a significant difference between any of the probabilities at the three context quantities (Table 7·8).

Conclusions

These results were considered to be fairly decisive. While there was plentiful evidence that a considerable amount of accurate prediction does occur, there was no indication that quantity of context beyond 5 or 6 words

Table 7·8. Combinations of variables ranking mean number of successful replacements in the same way as context quantity

Variables	Bilateral context quantity 5–6 words	11–12 words	19–20 words	n (No. of words per variable combination)
Formal language, content words:				
Mean	11·83	13·83	16·33	6
SD	17·42	18·84	6·77	
Written language, content word:				
Mean	11·00	15·50	16·00	6
SD	17·25	18·10	15·50	
Formal language, initial segment:				
Mean	17·50	28·50	32·25	4
SD	15·20	18·48	19·47	
Formal written language, initial segment:				
Mean	16·50	27·00	34·00	2
SD	12·02	12·73	22·63	
Formal spoken language, initial segment:				
Mean	18·50	29·50	30·50	2
SD	23·33	28·99	24·75	

bilaterally is a factor affecting predictability. It may of course be the case that particular words in particular types of context do become more predictable as the surrounding context increases; this study however suggests that such words and contexts will be exceptions to the general trend. This being the case, any argument for Cloze Procedure as a technique for assessing general proficiency in a language, or for assessing an important part of that general proficiency, based on that technique's presumed requirement of the subject that he use wide-ranging linguistic constraints in restoring deletions, must be seriously weakened. It is possible that the subject *does* use information from such constraints—but he does not *have* to.

SECTION II

Communicative Language Testing

8

Keynote paper

Communicative testing: jam tomorrow?

Andrew Harrison

"The rule is, jam to-morrow and jam yesterday—but never jam today."
"It *must* come sometimes to 'jam today',," Alice objected.
"No, it can't," said the Queen. "It's jam every *other* day: to-day isn't any *other* day, you know."
"I don't understand you," said Alice. "It's dreadfully confusing!"
(Carroll: Through the looking-glass)

The label "communicative" is used so often nowadays in connection with language learning materials that it is in danger of being taken for granted, like the supermarket label on the jam jar. But the quality of jam varies: we ought to look carefully at the product before buying to see whether we have whole fruit and sugar or fruit acid, glucose syrup, flavouring, and so on. If this wariness is necessary for courses and textbooks, how much more so for assessment material. The test jam jar is often opaque and we do not know what we have got until we try it. It ought to be possible however to establish what we should look for in the list of ingredients to distinguish the real thing from imitations. Here are three.

1. A communicative test should assess language used for a purpose beyond itself. An oral interview for example can be used to assess how well the learner can manipulate language in response to stereotyped questions, but a communicative version demands a response to circumstances. This rules out tests in which the learner is asked to display his language competence for no other reason than to have it assessed.

2. A communicative test should depend on the bridging of an information gap. It has to propose a language-using purpose which can be fulfilled by the communicative skill so far acquired by the learner. He must *need* to know or to tell—and his interlocutor must be in a similar necessity of explaining or finding out. For example, one kind of role play consists of

DVLPMNTS IN LANGUAGE TESTING
ISBN: 0-12-360880-5

reading out the alternative parts in a script; another could be planning a holiday on the basis of travel brochures. The former has no intrinsic value as a communication: the latter necessarily involves expression of information by one part to the exchange and understanding of it by the other. This approach rules out exchanges in which the questioner has no interest in the answer (e.g. "And how did you come to school this morning (not that I care)?").

3. A communicative test should represent an encounter. The situation at the end of it should be different from what it was at the beginning, and this means that there has to be some sequence within the test. It may require a simple transition from not knowing to knowing (e.g. understanding a text, whether written or spoken). A more complex transition would be from data given in one form to a conclusion reached in another, by way of several intermediary stages. The sequence in this case can be either putting together information contributed through several participants, as in jigsaw exercises and games, or building on several kinds of information supplied to one person, as in taking a phone message, looking something up in a reference book and leaving a written note. In this kind of exchange some personal commitment has to be made by the learner to the outcome of the communication, and the participants' real or assumed characters and attitudes will have rubbed off on one another to some extent, however small.

When these criteria are applied to test types, it appears that the difference between communicative tests and others is not the same as a contrast between traditional and modern—a throwing out of the old in favour of the newer—but a fresh starting point: purpose. The good old-fashioned translation is *out* as a means of showing what a student knows (or doesn't know) of the language, but is *in* for those who would be translators (as it always has been in the examinations of the Institute of Linguists). For the latter however the approach is different, and the marking criteria should be concerned more with applied semantics than with effective stylistics. On the other hand, the definitions given above exclude some types of test which are currently advocated and widely used, such as cloze and dictation. It is argued that these tests assess representations of linguistic modes of thinking (Oller, 1979), but they do not involve the student in any useful activity, even though they are pragmatic in the widest sense of being quick and convenient for classroom use (Cohen, 1981). They are chiefly a means of generating scores for linguistic artefacts in helpfully discriminating distributions. (This is not to say that they are not useful, merely that they are not communicative.) Attempts to apply cloze techniques to authentic situations are unsatisfactory because the damage done to the text has social connotations. Who wants to stay in a hotel so damp that parts of the notices on the wall are obscured by patches of mould? The sociolinguistic shortfall of cloze is however considerably more subtle than this, since it cannot accommodate the background information which is used by parties to a real communicative exchange—the "shared background expectancies" quoted and discussed by Johns-Lewis (1981).

Davies (1978) considers that attempts to assess communicative competence are likely merely to "provide a little more validity in the shape of examples of language use"; the rigours of reliability will not allow otherwise. Throw in a few real strawberries and the jam may not taste much different, but at least it will be better than before. The discussion above however suggests that the definition should be categorical rather than additive. A test type does not become communicative by mixing in a dash of reality: it is communicative because of the use made of it, and if it cannot be used to represent a communicative purpose, it cannot be a communicative test. The same technique faces different ways in different contexts: even reading aloud, which has been out of favour with modernists from Jespersen onwards, could offer useful evidence at an audition for newsreaders. The answer to the question: Is it communicative? depends on the circumstances and the ability of the test technique to fit them.

This circumstantial argument reflects back the notional/functional view of language learning: the student learns what is needed for predictable circumstances, and should be assessed similarly. It also suggests that the circumstances extend forward into other areas which are included in the vaguenesses of the term "ethnography". It is instructive to examine what happens in language learning outside EFL, not just ESL and EWL (English as a World Language) but English for young native learners, modern languages (i.e. French, German and so on, in schools and in adult education); and other subjects in the curriculum, from music to maths. In all these instances there are occasions when an applied communicative skill has to be assessed, and there may be helpful parallels in the way in which the problems are approached.

There are four issues which seem crucial in considering communicative testing: content, groups and individuals, judgements and realism.

The *specification of content* for any test should look forward to the use of results and back to the teaching. This is why the ELTDU scale (English Language Teaching Development Unit) is divided into sections, with the content of each depending on who is looking at it. Similarly, the communicative test is concerned both with functional learning and with the application by the student of what he has learnt to use outside language itself (Harrison, 1979). This implies that the communicative test is largely a proficiency test—but not entirely, since there must also be elements of achievement in it if it relates to the course which precedes it. This interplay between learning, the assessment and the real (even if only simulated) applications beyond is an essential element in communicative testing. A student who has not learnt how to apply what he has learnt to practical uses cannot be expected to tackle a communicative test. This application should be a deliberately planned part of the course, because it will not happen by some kind of linguistic metamorphosis at a given point in the student's progress. Informal assessments (probably not called 'tests" at all) should therefore be part of the learning programme, a constant source of feedback on the way in which students are developing these application skills (Sewell, 1976; Valette, 1974). This process can be considered as an aspect of methodology, a progress within the lesson from a learning phase into an assessment phase (Hayward et al. 1981), or as a gradual integration of parts into a whole (Fischer, 1981). There is no shortage of publications for communicative teaching, both courses and supplementary material such as authentic listening, drama in the classroom, games, simulations and problem solving. All these, as well as the better communicative course material, can offer strategies for assessment. Collections of teaching suggestions for particular groups of learners can also provide ideas for tests (Holden, 1977; Nott, 1977).

Teaching and testing have more in common than the rather sour comments of some teachers about tricks and traps (e.g. White, 1980) would have us believe. Good communicative tests (like other good tests) are straightforward tasks for the student to do, not Machiavellian sorting systems. Both *groups and individuals* are necessarily involved in communicative teaching, and should therefore also be the concern of communicative testing. Group oral examinations have been successfully run since 1953 by the English Speaking Board, whose first concern was spoken language for native speakers as a medium of self-development (Burniston, 1968) but now applies the same principles to EAL (English as an Acquired Language). Assessment of pairs of students also exists in school tests in modern languages (Clark, 1980). The real difficulties with group testing lie in the judgements to be made (see below) rather than setting up the discussion.

Concern with the individual student is a logical outcome of a needs approach, since each learner's needs will in theory be different from every other's. But individualized learning has more complex bases than this, and from the point of view of assessment implies testing the individual when ready. This leads on to concepts of mastery learning and criterion reference, both of which involve cross-currents of definition of goals, what constitutes success and organization of classes (Brown, 1980). The theories are easier to formulate than to put into practice, as the schemes of graded objectives in modern languages have discovered (Harding et al. 1980; Schools Council, 1983). Logical consequences include assessment profiles and self-assessment along the way, as in the *Tour de France* course (see

Johnstone, 1980) and the integration of assessment with tasks undertaken in class—there are parallels here in mathematics (Banks, 1981) and English in primary schools (Tough, 1979).

As always, two kinds of *judgement* are required in communicative testing—the pre-test one which makes objective marking possible and the post-test one which is subjective. If communication means the application of language in social contexts, the candidate cannot be asked in some objective way if he/she has understood: the understanding must be reflected in some purpose, if only "enjoyment". A joke may induce the student to smile, but until he/she has told the story to someone else there is no guarantee he/she has got the point. This principle rules out multiple-choice tests, both realistically, because they do not represent practical choices, and technically, because they are incestuously norm-referenced. Again, as with cloze, this is not to say that multiple-choice tests and other objective techniques based on the same principles have no value in assessment: it is just that they cannot be made communicative. The new Royal Society of Arts tests of reading skills ask for a demonstration of understanding, not for understanding as part of a progressive social relationship: the tests of writing do demand understanding of this kind however, as a necessary prelude to the expression of ideas. An objective test of communication relies on the resulting objects: a drawing done according to instructions (North West Regional Examinations Board, 1980), information extracted in response to requirements (Phillips, 1978); or on the resulting actions (Trinity College).

The assessment of live exchanges is probably the most urgent problem in communicative testing—like translation, it is impossible but essential. There are two basic principles on which these subjective judgements can be made: by category or by series. In the former, a total performance is assessed on various dimensions which are considered to contribute to the value of that performance. Assessments in oral examinations have almost traditionally been made in this way on the basis of categories such as vocabulary, grammar, pronunciation, fluency. The FSI scale and Carroll's banding system (B. J. Carroll, 1980) are refinements of this approach, but no different from it in principle. Its success depends more on what the descriptions of the categories mean to the assessors than on the content of the student's utterances, so that its main drawback is the necessity to train assessors with practical examples of what a given mark means—descriptions are not enough.

The other principle for the assessment of a student's performance is to regard it as a series of utterances, each of which is judged first for its communicative value and then for its appropriateness to the circumstances. In this case the assessor is a putative native speaker, involved in the same circumstances, and the crucial question is: what does he/she understand?

This is judging what has been called the "face value" of the utterance (Beardsmore and Renkin, 1971). A variation on this principle is to take as the unit not utterances, which in effect means semantic entities, but tone groups, which, it is claimed, can be objectively identified and marked quite mechanically (Ferguson, 1980). But this development takes too little account of sense, that is, of context.

If the needs approach, through functions and notions to applications, is to be logically followed through into assessment, the communicative exchange must be judged in its context. The basis must be the content of real exchanges, rather than speculation about what language in use may consist of, generalized into a mark scheme or scaling system. What does the fluent speaker have to do to get a particular communicative job done? The control necessary for reliable assessments should arise from the tasks which are to be achieved, the exchanges which are made, and the communicative problems which have been solved. One way of establishing these sequences is to find out by recording (and possibly transcribing) exactly what a fluent speaker says in the circumstances set by the test.

The problem then arises of how to assess on the wing: the group discussion goes on its way regardless of the assessor, and he must catch what he needs for his purposes as it goes by. But as with a paternoster lift, he can step on one of the passing platforms and progress up the building from floor to floor in stages, exploring each floor in turn. If the exchange goes along necessary (even if in detail unpredictable) lines, he can look for a particular factor at a given stage, but if he misses it there is always another platform coming by as a jumping on and off point for the next assessment. A necessary condition is that there are enough potential elements to be assessed for some to be omitted without affecting the sample of assessments actually made—a kind of testing redundancy which parallels linguistic redundancy, with much the same effect: the essentials are grasped with the help of contextual clues, only in the case of testing the clues have all been laid in advance, as in a good detective story.

Assessment of language exchanges in progress has parallels with the assessment of performance in music (Swanwick, 1981). There are the same problems of judging individual variations on a set task and comparing these with a notional "good performance" which in itself is a consensus of various possibilities, arrived at by experience of past performances.

Realism is the test situation. Various connotations of realism may be considered as aspects of assessment, such as the relationship of the task to be done with real life activities (is it the same, or only similar?); the plausibility of the role for the student (is this something he/she would do with language in a potential application, or is it all an act ?) the authenticity of the written or spoken text, and also of the intended response (is it what would occur in the context, or is it diluted in some way?). But these are somewhat esoteric questions, because the test situation *is*, like Gertrude Stein's rose; and whatever steps are taken to make it more realistic, it will nearly always be a representation, as the second halves of the bracketed questions in the previous sentence suggest. But then classroom activities are nearly always a representation too, and if tests need to be more like learning processes (as argued above), this is perhaps more important than their relationship with the world outside. Nevertheless, there are possibilities for real applications in learning: classroom transactions have their own validity (Clark, 1981) and other subjects can be taught through the medium of the foreign language (Widdowson, 1978; *sections bilingues* in Hawkins and Perren, 1978). As a real application of testing, the procedures through which students have necessarily to go on their first day at a language school can be used as the basis for a communicative assessment (Harrison, 1983). Outside activities can also be the occasion for language practice: jewellery-making, kites, pottery (Davis, 1977); exchanges of materials and cassettes by post (Jones, 1979; Landis, 1980); sports (summer course brochures, by implication); and of course games and puzzles of various kinds (Lee, 1979; Wright *et al.*, 1980; Geddes and Sturtridge, 1978; Maley and Grellet, 1981, among many others) and simulations (Jones, 1980; Sturtridge, 1977; Lynch, 1977; Wright, 1980 and 1981). The same techniques can be adapted for assessment purposes, and many of them could result in communicative tests.

All these are general applications, but more specialized, or specific uses of language can also be communicative in learning (Holden, 1977; Jupp and Hodlin, 1975; Moore, 1980) and texts of this kind often include suggestions for assessment techniques. The practice of professional or scientific skill can also result in assessable sequences, for example in medicine (Knox, 1975) or science (Shayer and Adey, 1981).

Some comments on future problems and possibilities—the content and labelling of tomorrow's jam?—are offered in conclusion.

Teachers are in general conservative, happier with what is familiar than with new bandwagons (Harrison, 1980). Where they are not, or are pushed into innovation by higher authority, teacher training is vital. This is a truism on the classroom front: it applies equally to teachers' understanding of the place of assessment in communicative learning.

Rubric is crucial in communicative testing. The problem is how to explain to the student what he/she is meant to do in a communicative test without long explanations in the foreign language, which risk being more difficult to understand than the text chosen for comprehension. The answer must be familiarity: students need practice, not in the old sense of how to get through the external examination (training in content) but how to use in practical situations what has been learnt in more limited contexts (application and transfer).

Testing is traditionally associated with exactitude, but it is not an exact science. Needs-based specifications may clear new ground, but they can be carried through into practice only with considerable difficulty. For example, the single typical exemplar of a language user is not necessarily typical of any of the groups to which he/she belongs, and analysis of even this one individual's contexts of operation is exceedingly complicated. At the other end of the procedure, in the evaluation of responses, it is likely that old notions of error will die hard (Fox, 1979). The quantities resulting from test-taking look like exact figures—69 per cent looks different from 68 per cent but cannot be so for practical purposes, though test writers may imply that they are distinguishable by working out tables of precise equivalences of test and level, and teachers may believe them. These interpretations of scores are inappropriate even for traditional testing but for communicative testing they are totally irrelevant. The outcome of a communicative test is a series of achievements, not a score denoting an abstract concept of "level".

"A great deal of discourse is routinized and yet the exchange of meanings is a creative process in which language is only one symbolic resource among others; so the conceptual framework is rhetoric rather than logic and the grammar one of choices rather than rules" (Ager, 1981; Halliday, 1978). This approach should be applied to assessments, but the problem is how to judge the appropriateness of rhetoric and the correctness of choices in the social context set by a communicative test.

New developments in the theory of language testing since Lado have been slow because the production and statistical justification of multiple-choice tests has made other more subjective assessments look weak by comparison. Yesterday it was difficult to sort out what to test (how was a specification to be drawn up, by lists of vocabulary? and if so, which words and on what basis? and/or by selections of structures? if so, which and why?). But it was easy to set the tests, with a logical system of test formats and statistically respectable results. Of its kind, this could be jam of high quality. Today it is theoretically easy to specify what is wanted in communicative tests: simply the language needed to exchange meanings in contexts. But in practice the meanings and contexts have to be defined, and that is a problem which has not so far been solved. Equally problematical is how to assess reliably enough and how to know that this sufficient level of reliability has been reached. The standard techniques, based on the spread provided by a normal distribution, will not do. The jam's ingredients—both validity fruit and reliability sugar— are obscured by the opaque pot called communication. We are not yet in a position to claim that communicative tests are better than the more familiar varieties, but we have to work on the assumption that they will be, tomorrow. In the meantime, we need to examine the labels.

> Chivers Hartley . . . have already brought out their new range, Extra Jam . . . 13p more expensive than their ordinary New Jam (will they now rename it Old Jam?). When we carried out taste tests in 1974, though, many people had difficulty in telling apart high and lower fruit content jams—so don't assume that 'extra jam' will automatically taste better.
>
> *Which?* November 1981

9

Response to Harrison

Who needs jam?

J. Charles Alderson

One of the interesting things about the analogy comparing communicative language tests to jam is that it is possible to pursue the analogy further than Harrison does to point out that jam is not necessarily itself a desirable product, since it is said to be fattening, bad for one's teeth, and so on. One might reasonably ask, then, who needs or wants jam? and equally, who needs or wants communicative language tests? There are at least three conceivable answers to this question.

1. "Teachers do, because they are doing communicative language teaching and they need the tests to go with the teaching". But if they *are* doing communicative teaching, the development of communicative achievement and progress tests should be no problem: all they have to do is sample the syllabus. So if the syllabus *is* communicative, the tests must be too. If the tests aren't, then perhaps the syllabus isn't communicative *either*. The labels on the jars of communicative teaching need as much close examination as the test jam jar labels.

2. "Users need communicative tests because existing tests do not predict one's ability to communicate in the real world." However, we need to ask whether this is true, since the evidence, is at best scant. Yet even if it were true it would not in itself be an argument for communicative tests, but for better tests, better predictors. If existing tests are not good enough (and this refers to proficiency tests above all) then we need to ask whether this is because they are not communicative or because they are not good tests.

3. Academics want communicative tests because they feel that tests should relate more to what we know, now about language in use and communication. In other words, tests should correspond more closely

DVLPMNTS IN LANGUAGE TESTING
ISBN: 0-12-360880-5

to our theories of language use. Yet tests are merely (or at least in part) *operationalizations* of theories: theories put into practice implicitly or explicitly. Now if the operationalizations have not yet proved to be satisfactory, the fault may be not in the operationalizing but in the theory—it does not allow for operationalizations, because it is inadequate, incomplete or simply too vague. Perhaps when deploring the lack of communicative (proficiency) *tests* we should take a closer, more critical look at the *theories* of language in communication.

Perhaps the most important point to emerge from Harrison's paper is the warning not to accept as communicative any and every test that claims to be. This is a sensible and necessary warning that I endorse, and that accords with time-honoured testing practice: do not believe that a test is a test of X because it is called a test of X. And the validation of tests to determine whether a test *is* a test of X, is a reasonably well understood process. When setting up claims about what a test measures, it is essential to ask how one is going to *establish* the validity—what the *validation procedures* will be. The retort to any claim that 'This is a communicative language test" is "How do you know?" or "How do you propose to establish that claim as a fact?"

One of the objections to "traditional" testing practice is that it has concentrated on empirical, statistical validation at the expense of construct, content and above all face validity. The riposte, of course, is that "communicative testers" only talk about face validity, at the expense of other validities.

Harrison's paper assumes that we know what communicative language tests are, that we know what ingredients should be stated, in what proportions, on the label. But I suggest that we do not know this, we do not know yet what makes a test communicative, and we *need* theory to clarify for us what the defining characteristics of a communicative language test might be. In other words, when is a communicative language test not a communicative language test?

Harrison's paper states that "It is theoretically easy to specify what is wanted in communicative language tests: simply the language needed to exchange meaning in context." Yet this seems to me far too simplistic, and I hope to show that it is *not* theoretically easy to specify this: if it were we could *have* the tests already.

I propose first to comment on the three issues Harrison raises in the first part of his paper, that :

1. "A communicative test should assess language used for a purpose beyond itself."
2. "A communicative test should depend on the bridging of an information gap."
3. "A communicative test should represent an encounter."

These issues I see as being essentially inter-related, and depending upon the issues of purpose and authenticity. When Harrison calls for realism, for real life tasks, he is in fact talking about authenticity.

Now it is important to see that a test and the testing situation is an Activity Type in its own right—it has its own defining characteristics, its own rules and purposes. The purposes of participants in this Activity Type have their own "validity", their own authenticity. The testee can be seen to be *displaying* his ability or language for its assessment by an outsider. This makes language tests more similar to other tests, like music examinations, than to language use in the so-called "real-world". In his second Ingredient, Harrison refers to the participant's need to communicate—but what the participant *really* needs to communicate is his ability or knowledge, and anything else is clearly subsidiary, and simulated. So when considering Information Gaps, the true information gap, which exists for *all* tests, is what the testee "transmits" to the tester: The tester does not *know* the ability or knowledge of the testee, and it is this gap that both endeavour to fill—indeed, interesting research could be done by examining the way in which such information is communicated, in which meaning is created and negotiated during such an encounter. But this is tantamount to saying that *all* tests, not just "communicative language tests", contain Harrison's ingredients—they are purposive, bridge information gaps, and represent encounters. Indeed, I find it difficult to imagine *any* test which is purposeless in the sense I have just defined, which does not attempt to bridge a gap, and which does not represent an encounter. Moreover, I do not regard the bridging of information gaps as essential characteristics of communicative language tests, any more than communication can be seen as merely the *transfer* of information, unless information is defined in a very general sense indeed. The view of communication represented by the notion of gap-bridging implies that gaps can be and are bridged, that information is contained in chunks and that all that happens is that it is transferred. Yet surely another view of communication is at least imaginable, and plausible: namely, that meaning is neither transferred nor extracted, but is created by participants, is negotiated in encounters, and remains vague, undefined to the outside world but private to each participant and doubtless different for each. The "information gap" view of communication is at best partial, at worst wrong.

Harrison mentions four crucial issues in communicative language testing—test content, groups and individuals, judgements and realism—and I shall comment on these briefly:

1. *Test content*. This crucially depends upon Test Purpose, which is not mentioned: the What is affected by the Why of testing. Now it has already been argued that if the purpose is achievement testing the problem of the *what*, the test content, is not exclusively confined to testers: an achieve-

ment test samples the syllabus, quite simply, and the onus is on the teaching and the syllabus to specify test content. Thus this is *not* a crucial issue for communicative language tests that are syllabus related, although it is indeed a problem for proficiency tests.

2. *Groups and individuals.* This I see as non-controversial—group interactions need to be assessed. The real problem lies in the related issue of specification of what purposes individuals have to use language for, and Harrison himself touches upon the problems of needs analysis. The slogan that "The test should fit the learners" is fine, but learners vary enormously. We are here faced with the problem familiar from ESP testing: the tension between maximizing commonalities on the one hand, thereby moving away from specific purposes or maximizing individual differences and thereby moving away from measurement, which requires replicability. One solution that has been proposed is to eschew target situation and target performance analysis and go for the underlying target competence, the "enabling skills". The problem is that we stand before an abyss of ignorance of the nature and contribution of such abilities, skills and competences.

3. *Judgements.* The first point, a relatively minor one, is that I do not see why multiple choice tests "cannot be made communicative". Multiple choice is just a technique like any other, and can surely serve a variety of purposes. Multiple-choice tests can be designed to produce a range of different tests. If Harrison means that in real life we are not faced by four choices when producing or processing language then I can only say that this is a face validity argument and as trivial as the argument that cloze tasks are "non-communicative" because in real life we do not read notices spotted with damp. The point is that if your criteria for validation are theoretical, rather than simple references to "realism"—and I've referred above to the limitations of the authenticity argument—then it is clearly possible to say that when communicating people have to predict, say, based on expectancies about the communication, then seek to confirm these predictions. A test derived from this theory, as a cloze test might be, could well be called communicative, from a construct validity point of view.

The second point is somewhat more important and it relates to judgements: who is to make them and why and how? What is an acceptable performance in a "communicative" situation? Acceptable to whom? And having found our "fluent native speaker", where are we to find his/her criteria for acceptable and appropriate behaviour? How do we account for (a) individual variation in standards and prescriptions, (b) tolerance of ambiguity, of deviance and linguistic variation?

Native speakers clearly vary in their own abilities: are we to take account of this variation? How might this be done? Must we delay designing tests until we have completed the research? Clearly not, but it seems to me somewhat unjustified to assume that judgements of acceptability and appropriacy can be safely made already on the basis of what we know about language, language in use and the necessary and sufficient abilities that underly communicative performances.

4. *Realism.* I have already commented on authenticity and the problems of defining authentic test tasks. Harrison usefully mentions ways in which classroom situations can be used to authenticate, or rather to produce more realistic simulations. The plea for realism is essentially a plea for face validity, and I think Harrison has a point—we do need tests that have greater face validity, especially for the testee, but also for interested lay people like sponsors and users. It is important, nevertheless, to remember that, even if one might wish to make the extreme claim that it is the *most* important criterion, it is *not* the *only* one. The most important question to be asked of any test, is: What is it measuring? As suggested, this can be determined by a variety of means including face inspection.

Having achieved a description of what a test is measuring—itself not an unproblematic task—we then need to evaluate that description in terms of what *should* be measured.

The criteria for helping one answer those questions come from theory, from what one knows and believes about language and communicative abilities, and from what one knows and believes about communication with and through language. Like it or not, we need theory to help us decide when a communicative language test is or is *not* a communicative language test.

Any test is both an elicitation procedure, and an assessment procedure. A test is composed of Task and of Criteria, and to advance in communicative language testing we need to consider both aspects: what tasks shall testees be given? How should we decide which to select or contrive? Which skills need to be elicited and which are best elicited by which task?

We also need to ask: which aspects of task performance are we to look at? Are we to judge analytically or globally? What is the range of possible judgements, for given test purposes? And of course the old testing problem—how are we to make such judgements moderately consistently? In "Issues in Language Testing" I outlined four main areas of concern that one should consider when asking whether any *language* test is measuring what it should measure. We should at lest consider the test's (any test's) view of *language*; its view of the *learner*; its view of *language learning* and its view of *background knowledge* (Alderson and Hughes, Eds, 1982: 50–52). It seems to me that much of the debate over communicative testing is very limited in its scope, and as I have said, has a very limited view of what communication is or might be and what might be involved in learning to communicate. We need to broaden the debate to include more factors when considering test validity—the validity of *any* test—but particularly and crucially for communicative tests.

As I see it, the Way Forward in this area of testing is not through dogma, nor through the paralysis of doubt but by honest attempts to answer questions, like those I have asked in this Response. We need to gather more and better information in appropriate areas where we are presently ignorant, but we should not be afraid of admitting ignorance. When discussing the way forward, however, we need to be sure (or to believe) that we know where "forward" is, and that we actually want and need to move. To return to Harrison's metaphor: who wants jam? Some people might prefer strawberry jam to gooseberry jam, others might not want anything sweet but would prefer marmalade or peanut butter. Perhaps others don't want any kind of spread—they would prefer bread and cheese or pheasant or toad in the hole.

If I may end with a quotation myself, from Alice in Wonderland. Appropriately this is a conversation between the Cheshire Cat and Alice— appropriate because the Cheshire Cat was renowned for disappearing before one's very eyes, at most inconvenient moments just as do discussions on communicative language testing, also mysteriously and inconveniently:

"Which way? Which way?", asked Alice.
"It all depends on where you want to go," replied the Cheshire Cat.

10

Assessment of pupil achievement in the independent evaluation of *Tour de France*

Brian Parkinson

The first part of this paper presents the background to an attempt at assessing the global performance of pupils following the Scottish National French course for the 12–14 age group, *Tour de France*. It briefly discusses some of the problems and issues which arose. The second part of the paper consists of the marking scheme which was developed, and the paper concludes with some specimen marking sheets.

Background and issues

Tour de France was piloted in 44 schools throughout Scotland in the period 1979–1981. The testing of pupils near the end of the course formed one of the four main parts of the empirical work of evaluation, alongside lesson observation, teacher interview and teacher questionnaire, and involved all pupils in the pilot classes of 30 schools (average approximately 60 pupils per school).

The aim of this part of the evaluation was not to pass judgement on individual pupils, teachers or schools, but to make general statements about the performance of pupils in pilot classes on a variety of tasks. It was thus unnecessary for any one pupil to make more than a small fraction of the various items and versions of the various tests, etc., but the allocation of pupils to items was such that statistically valid generalizations could be made about performance in specified domains.

The requirements of test construction for the purpose of curriculum evaluation (a purpose sadly neglected in foreign language testing methodology) are clearly rather different from those encountered in testing for the certification or other treatment of individuals. In testing of the latter kind it

DVLPMNTS IN LANGUAGE TESTING
ISBN: 0-12-360880-5

is sometimes possible to "get away with" norm-referenced assessment generating a single mark, and appeal to supposed common understanding of the meaning of e.g. a "Pass" or a "Grade A"; but a detailed understanding of the outcomes of a particular course can be obtained only from criterion-referenced testing yielding detailed profiles of pupil achievement.

Our tests attempted to generate profiles revealing both the extent to which the *discrete elements* in the offered *language syllabus* (lexical items, morpho-syntactic rules, etc.) had been mastered, and the *general nature and adequacy* of *global performance* in selected semantic and situational areas, having regard to all dimensions likely to be relevant to successful language use. The first of these two aspects of performance is relatively unproblematic, and the relevant parts of our test battery, which followed well established models, are not reported here. For the assessment of global performance, however, it was found necessary to tread relatively uncharted ground, and some of the problems and issues arising are now discussed, with special reference to "Test 2" of the battery, an interactive oral test involving replies to a series of personal questions (Part 1) followed by a role-play task, cued in L1, where the testee was required to take the initiative to achieve certain transactional goals (Part 2).

The marking scheme for Test 2 attempted to take into account most of the dimensions for the analysis of communicative performance mentioned in Carroll (1978), with modifications reflecting the characteristics of the task and population.

The main debate within the research group was on the extent to which numerical scales should be used in the analysis. It was generally agreed that the uninformative 1–100 type overall scale should be discarded in favour of a system describing performance in 7–10 Carroll-type dimensions, but I originally envisaged within these categories scales of up to 9 points. Colleagues argued that such marks would be unreliable and of uncertain meaning, and leaned in the direction of purely nominal categories, representing different types of error, with no hierarchical ordering except that between "fully acceptable", "less than fully acceptable", and perhaps "totally unacceptable". As will be seen, the present system is a compromise between the two positions; the general question of the appropriate place of scaling and of nominal category descriptions in this type of assessment merits further exploration.

Another important issue was the extent to which credit should be given for the "reeling off" of learnt holophrases. An "interlanguage" approach such as that advocated in Corder (1981) would imply that production of such holophrases says little about mastery of the language system, and that more credit should be given for apparently original synthesized utterances, even if (or even because) containing errors. We concluded, however, that a functional/communicative approach implies recognition of the value of holophrases, and that the ability to produce these in *appropriate discourse sequences* is a non-trivial accomplishment which deserves recognition as part of a wider "proxeogrammatical competence". We suggest that the modification of interlanguage theory to embrace the insights of functional/ discourse-oriented approaches is an urgent task for applied linguists. In our marking system, credit could be gained by appropriate use of learnt phrases, although mechanically holophrastic answers were normally penalised on the complexity/range dimension.

It was found possible to operationalize all the categories listed, and in the limited number of reliability trials which proved possible reasonable inter-coder agreement was established. In most cases, the chosen categories were also felt to have captured the important information on pupil performance, but with hindsight one additional category, *transactional coherence*, was felt necessary for Part 2; this would deal with those pupils who, whilst perhaps speaking accurately, relevantly, politely, etc. failed to carry out all parts of the intended task (e.g. asking the "shopkeeper" for the price of twenty items, buying none) or realized the correct functions in incorrect order (praxeogrammatical errors).

The results of Test 2 are not yet available (they will appear in Parkinson *et al.* (1983)), but it is already clear that the test was useful, in conjunction with the discrete item tests, in providing a coherent account of what pupils could do after two years of the course. We feel that the marking system offers a promising model for the criterion-referenced assessment of communicative competence, although further refinement and validation of the categories will be needed.

Marking scheme for Test 2

Part 1

General. The pupil response to each question should be assessed on each of the dimensions of *basic message communication, size, phonetic accuracy, morpho-syntactic accuracy, complexity/range, speed/hesitation,* and *need for repetition/independence.* "Question" is defined as each of the numbered divisions of Part 1. "Response" is everything which the pupil said, analysed where appropriate in relation to what the tester said.

General criteria for the award of marks in each category are as given below, and additional ground rules and examples for particular questions are given in the accompanying specimen marking sheets.

Where no assessment can be made of a particular response in a particular dimension, either because of a general ground rule or because of particular features of the individual response, an asterisk should be inserted in the relevant cell. For example, a zero response should be awarded (0) for "basic message" and "size", (*) for other dimensions; and a response consisting of an English proper name would normally receive (*) on the two "accuracy" dimensions. If a pupil is deemed not to have had a chance to answer a question at all, or to expand his/her answer, (*) may also be awarded, in the first case on all dimensions, in the second for "size" and "complexity/range".

Marking criteria for each category

Basic message

(0) It is likely that a native speaker would not have been able to extract from the response any message which could be considered a reasonable answer to the question.

(2) It is likely that a native speaker would have been able to extract such a message.

(1) This category is used for doubtful or marginal cases. It should be used very sparingly, and if it has to be invoked a note should be made of the nature of the doubt or marginality.

If a pupil produces two or more utterances, each apparently intended to convey separate items of information, he/she should be given a separate "basic message" mark for each. "Utterance" is defined as the realization in "parole" of a sentence or main clause in "langue"; a second or subsequent utterance is held to exist if a second finite verb is used, or a finite verb repeated (other than in self-correction or hesitation phenomena); or if the pupil takes a new turn; or if pauses and/or intonation contours make clear that he has finished one "complete thought" and started another, but a list of noun phrases counts as a single utterance, and "oui", "non", "yes", "no", "pardon" etc. are not separately marked. Thus "Nous mangeons des frites et des pommes." is one utterance, whereas "Nous mangeons des frites. Nous mangeons des pommes." is two utterances. Similarly "des frites (pause) des pommes" is one utterance, but "dans la mer. a la plage." is two utterances.

Size. The number of words is recorded. The definition of "word" is generous, so that "il y a" is 3 words, "j'aime" is 2, but hesitation phenomena ("er", "um") and false starts clearly marked as such and replaced with something else are ignored.

Phonetic accuracy

(0) The pronunciation is so incorrect that it is barely possible for the

marker (and perhaps impossible for a native speaker) to recognize what form is being attempted.

(1) The pronunciation is highly inaccurate and "un-French" but not as bad as in (0).

(2) The utterance contains definite mistakes of pronunciation beyond those allowed in (3), but is none the less generally satisfactory in this respect.

(3) The phonetic accuracy approximates to the highest level normally expected of the foreign learner. There is no failure to make basic phonemic distinctions e.g. between /u/ and /y/, nor in presence or absence of nasalization, nor in general shape of intonation contours. The awarding of this mark is not disqualified by use of alveolar /r/ or dark /l/ or by minor divergencies from the native standard in the shape of intonation contours and speech rhythms, in the closeness of close vowels or in the degree of lip-rounding on back vowels (provided that phonemic distinctions are made).

Where two or more utterances have been separately coded for "basic message", they are also separately coded for this dimension. A short, phonetically very simple utterance will normally be marked (0) or (3); only when more evidence is available will the intermediate categories by used. Thus category (3) does not imply "good French accent", but only "nothing wrong within the limits of this question".

Morpho-syntactic accuracy

(0) The utterance is entirely pidginized, with no syntactic markers, and no grammatical (closed-set) morphemes, including personal pronouns, or totally incorrect use of such markers as are present (e.g. third person for first).

(1) The utterance shows some evidence of the French morphosyntactic rule-system, the use of which is not totally incorrect, but the structure in general is highly inaccurate and "un-French".

(2) The utterance contains at least one error of morphology or syntax, but is none the less generally satisfactory in this respect.

(3) The utterance is totally correct in morpho-syntactic terms.

Where two or more utterances have been separately coded for "basic messages", they are also separately coded for this dimension. A short, structurally very simple utterance is normally coded (0) or (3) as above.

Complexity/range. This dimension is invoked only for answers containing more than one utterance, but a single coding is made for the whole answer.

(0) Utterances are produced according to a single pattern of the minimum complexity necessary to answer the question, resulting in a

degree of repetition unnatural in normal discourse (e.g. j'aime le football, j'aime le rugby, j'aime le hockey).
(2) The degree of variety between utterances is sufficient to make the answer acceptable in normal discourse.
(1) Used for doubtful or marginal cases, with note—cf. Basic Message.

Speed/hesitation. A single coding is made for the whole answer, as follows:
(0) The answer is produced so slowly, as a result of delay in starting and/or pauses within the answer, that if transferred to a real life context it would probably cause a breakdown of communication. In a single-utterance answer, a single delay of 8 seconds, or total delays of 15 seconds, should normally result in this coding, although discretion can be applied in unusual circumstances: in multiple-utterance answers, the time limits should be proportionately higher.
(1) The answer is produced slowly enough for there to be a likelihood of serious impairment of communication, but not slowly enough for a coding of (0).
(2) The speed of answer is sufficient for satisfactory interaction with a reasonably tolerant native speaker, but still outside the normal range of speeds of fluent native speakers.
(3) The speed of utterance is within the normal range of fluent native speakers.
In cases of failure to answer followed by prompts, the "hesitation" in the initial failure is not counted.

Need for repetition/independence. A single coding is made for the whole answer as follows:

(1) No repetition or prompting is needed to produce the answer.
(T) The answer is produced only after translation of the question.
(R) The answer is produced only after repetition of the question.
(B) The answer is produced only after tester offers first word or words of required answer.
(P) The answer is produced only after other prompt.
These categories may be combined, e.g. (R, R, T) means answer is produced after two repetitions and a translation. Notes should be made on more complex cases.

Part 2 (Interactive task)

The pupil response is marked on the dimensions of *basic message communication, size, phonetic accuracy, morpho-syntactic accuracy, speed/*

hesitation, *initiation*, *responsiveness* and *social appropriacy*. The first five of these are coded as for Part 1.

Initiation This is a measure of the extent to which the pupil responded to the teacher's injunction to "take the initiative" in role-play. A single coding is made for the whole answer. (0) is awarded if all pupil utterances are responses to specific tester questions or other prompts. (1) indicates that the pupil initiates an exchange sometimes, but not as much as in (2), which means that the pupil initiates all exchanges (excluding any cases where the tester makes initiation practically impossible—e.g. by immediately following answer with cross-question).

Responsiveness. This is also coded only once per pupil, and is an indication of the extent to which pupil utterances show awareness of, and ability to respond appropriately to, information contained in tester utterances. This includes, for example, not asking for vegetables which the "shop-keeper" has said he does not have, and answering cross-questions ("Et toi?" etc.). (0) is awarded for failure to give any indication of appropriate response, (2) for responses which are fully appropriate, in the sense that they display, or are not inconsistent with, comprehension of what needs to be comprehended, and that an attempt is made to answer questions etc. (although the answers need not be formally or socially correct). (1) is awarded if the pupil is "responsive" in some but not all cases, (*) if there is no opportunity to demonstrate responsiveness.

Social appropriacy. This is an indication of the extent to which the pupil conforms to the expected social norms of the role he/she is taken. It is mainly a question of the appropriate use of "Bonjour", "Au revoir", "monsieur/madame", "s'il vous plaît" and "merci", although other features, such as the inappropriate use of "C'est cher!", may be taken into consideration if the marker deems them relevant to the social acceptability of the pupil's performance. In Task D, an informal style will be acceptable, but a formal style will not be penalized. (0) is awarded in cases of total failure to produce these indications of appropriacy, (1) for partially correct use, (2) for totally correct use.

The following charts show model codings for selected pupil answers to selected questions in Test 2, with comments where necessary.

Specimen Marking Sheets for Test 2, Part 1. Questions A1, A2, B2

A1 (etc.) Comment t'appelles-tu? A2 (etc.) Quel âge as-tu? B2 (etc.) Où habites-tu?

Answer	Basic message	Size	Phonetic	Morpho-syntactic	Complexity/ range	Speed/ hesitation	Inde-pendence	Comment
A1								
(1) Je m'appelle George	2	4	3	3	*	3	1	
(2) Je m'appelle . . . Gavin	2	4	3	3	*	2	1	
A2								
(1) J'ai quatre ans	0	4	3	3	*	3	1	
(2) . . . Treize ans	2	2	3	3	*	2	1	
B2								
(1) J'habite Menstrie en Ecosse	2	5	3	3	*	3	1	
(2) J'habite à Glasgow en Ecosse	2	6	3	3	*	3	1	

Specimen Marking Sheets for Test 2, Part 1. Questions A3, A4

A3 Qu'est-ce que tu aimes manger? A4 Qu'est-ce que tu n'aimes pas manger?

Answer	Basic message	Size	Phonetic	Morpho-syntactic	Complexity/range	Speed/hesitation	Inde-pendence	Comment
A3								
(1)								
P. Pardon?	2	4	1	3	*	1	RT	
T. (repeats and translates)								
P. . . . des . . . cravettes								
. . . des . . . fritz								
(2) . . . em . . . aime manger des chocolats et des gâteaux	2	7	3	2	*	2	1	
A4								
(1)								
P. . . . je n'ai mange pas . . . le crabe	2	10	3	1	*	1	1	
T. Oui								
P. . . . Et la, et le . . . . . . et le l'oignon, et l'oignon /lɔny/	2		0	2		1		
(2) N'aime pas manger le frite	2	6	3	1	*	3	1	

Specimen Marking Sheets for Test 2, Part 1. Questions A5, A6

A5 Qu'est-ce que tu aimes faire pendant les vacances? A6 Toi et tes copains/copines (écossais(es)) qu'est-ce que vous faites le soir?

Answer	Basic message	Size	Phonetic	Morpho-syntactic	Complexity/range	Speed/hesitation	Inde-pendence	Comment
A5								
(1)								
T. (repeats and translates)					*	1	RT	
P. en (mon?) la bicyclette . . . je joue au rugby et la . . . fussball, football	2	11	2	2				
(2)								
T. (translates)							T	
P. Dans le vacance aime faire . . . dans le vacance aime jouer à la plage	2	18	3	2	2	1		
T. Oui								
P. Et nage dans l'eau . . . et . . . et jouer . . . et joue avec ma copine	2		3	2				
A6								
(1)								
T. (repeat and partial translation)		8			0	1	RT	
P. . . . je joue au basket	1		3	3				"nous" needed for full basic message mark
. . . je monte l'autobus	1		3	3				
(2) lisez-uh lis et écouter les disques	1	6	2	2	*	2	1	

Specimen Marking Sheets for Test 2, Part 1. Question A7

Parle-moi un peu de ton collège s'il te plaît.

Answer	Basic message	Size	Phonetic	Morpho-syntactic	Complexity/range	Speed/hesitation	Inde-pendence	Comment
A7								
(1)								
P. Ici?	2	50	3	*	2	2	1	
T. Oui								
P. . . . le matin je faire le	2		3	2				
gâteau et après la								
travail dans la classe								
de géographie et la	2		3	2				
class d'anglais								
il a beaucoup de classe	2		3	1				
dans la collège . . . il								
a beaucoup de profs.	2		3	2				
J'aime français et								
anglais et je n'aime	2		3	1				
pas la musique . . .	2		3	3				
j'aime la gymnastique	2		3	3				
(2)		16						
j'aime la géographie. . .	2		2	3	2	1	1	
er. . . . les mathématiques								
/-S/. . .								
je déteste les musique . . .	2		3	1				
je n'aime pas la français	2		3	2				

Specimen Marking Sheets for Test 2, Part 1. Version A

Situation: Tester = shopkeeper (food); pupil = customer. "Ask me the price of a few things, tell me how much or how many you want and pay for them." (For this example, only first part marked for BM, Phonetic, Morpho-syntactic; whole question marked on other dimensions.)

Answer	Basic message	Size	Phonetic	Morpho-syntactic	Speed/hesitation	Initiation	Responsive	Appropriacy	Comment
(1)									
P. Un kilo de . . . un kilo de l'oignon, s'il te plait	2	60	3	1	1	1	2	1	"Size excludes English utterances and repetitions. Needs to be correct only within 10%
T. qu'est-ce									
P. pardon?									
T. qu'est—er—un kilo de l'oignon, qu'est-ce que tu (7 secs)									
T. un kilo d'oignons monsieur, oui monsieur, voila.									
P. Er, merci, er (5 secs) . . . qu'est-ce que tu (X2) . . . I'm trying to ask how much but I can't remember.									
T. (. . .) Oui, un kilo de l'oignons c'est deux francs									
P. Oui, voilà deux francs	2		3	3					
T. Merci monsieur									
P. (2 secs) un livre de pommes de terre et un livre de bananes	2		3	2					
T. Oui monsieur, les pommes de terre voila, et les bananes, voila									
(etc.)									
P. Oui									
T. You want to say combien,									
P. Combien									
T. 4F, 10 monsieur									
P. Oui, c'est 4, voilà le 4F 10									
T. Merci monsieur									
P. Il fait beau									
T. Oui, il fait beau, n'est-ce pas									

(Approx. 15 more lines not reproduced here)

Version A (contd)

Answer	Basic message	Size	Phonetic	Morpho-syntactic	Speed/hesitation	Initiation	Responsive	Appropriacy	Comment
(2)									
P. Bonjour, monsieur	2	70	3	*	3	2	2	2	Unclear if /rɔb/ is false start or attempt at separate item
T. Bonjour, madame									
P. Il fait beau, n'est-ce pas?	2		3	3					
T. Ah oui, il fait beau									
P. Vous avez des pommes?	2		3	3					
T. Oui madame	1		1	3					
P. Et des /rɔb/, des oranges									
T. Oui madame, nous avons des oranges									
P. C'est combien de pommes?									
T. Les pommes, c'est, c'est er, un franc 30 le kilo			(etc.)						
P. Deux kilos s.v.p.									
T. Deux kilos de pommes, madame. Voilà									
P. Merci. Et vous avez des pommes de terre?									
T. Oui, on les vend par (?) cinq kilo									
P. Un demo-kilo s.v.p.									
T. Un demi-kilo!? Une livre de pommes de terre! Bon									
P. Merci									
T. Voilà									
P. Vous avez des poires aujourd'hui?									
T. Oui madame, je crois Ah oui, voilà									

(Approx. 10 more lines not reproduced here)

Specimen Marking Sheets for Test 2, Part 1. Version D

T = pen-friend's cousin. "Ask me anything at all about myself."

Answer	Basic message	Size	Phonetic	Morpho-syntactic	Speed/Hesitation	Initiation	Responsive	Appropriacy	Comment
(1)									
P. Bonjour monsieur	2	12	3	3	2	2	*	1	"Monsieur" not necessary in this question, but not wrong either.
T. Bonjour monsieur									
P. Comment t'appeles-tu?	2		3	3					
T. Je m'appelle François									
P. Où habitez-vous?	2		3	3					Finally "drying up" does not reduce "speed" mark, but does reduce "appropriacy".
T. J'habite à Cadroc en Bretagne	1		3	3					
P. . . . Parlez-vous écossais?									"Tu" or "vous" acceptable here, but appropriacy mark lost for inconsistency.
T. Non, je parle français et allemand, c'est tout									
P. (30 secs)									
T. Oh we'll leave that one									
(2)									
P. Comment t'appelles-tu?	2	46	3	3	2	2	*	1	
T. Je m'appelle François									
P. Ah bon! Quelle musique préférer François	2		2	1					
T. Oh, je préfère la musique classique									
P. Ah oui. Quel âge as-tu?	2		3	3					
T. J'ai 17 ans									
P. Ah. Tu as des frères, des soeurs?	2		3	3					
T. Non (. . .) je suis enfant unique									
P. Qu'est-que/vaton/père —eh. . . tu as . . . em. . . quelle materière prefere a—ou collège?	0		1	0					
	2		3	1					
T. Oh je préfère le latin et les maths									
P. Tu préfères—tu aimes le science?	2		3	2					
T. Oui, comme ci comme ça									
P. J'adore le science	2		3	2					
T. Oui?									
P. Au revoir	2	3							

SECTION III

Testing Language for Specific Purposes

11

Keynote paper

Issues in the testing of language for specific purposes

Brendan Carroll

The aim of this paper is to present some of the issues which have had to be identified and clarified in the process of devising tests which attempt to incorporate systematically non-linguistic features of the job or disciplines for which the tests were being prepared. It would be presumptuous to assume that even these modest purposes have yet been achieved.

The alternative approaches to language testing

It seems to me that there are two main and opposing points of entry to the devising of tests of linguistic behaviour reflecting two divergent points of view about language teaching. The first, which I will label the "Linguistic" approach, starts with the selection of the linguistically described items of grammar and lexis and assesses the behaviour in terms of its conformity to native-speaker norms. The second, which I will label the "Communicative" approach, starts with a specification of the socio-linguistic demands of particular settings and assesses the behaviour in terms of its communicative value.

This is not to say that the Linguistic approach necessarily ignores the demands of particular situations, or that the Communicative approach fails to consider features of linguistic usage. The difference lies rather in the point of entry and the sequence of specification, so that the final product need not be of entirely different natures. For example, a linguistically devised test of plurals and comparison could be set in the situation of the auction room, a communicatively devised test based on the process of auctioneering could well include items to test the mastery of plural and comparison forms. It all depends upon which are the independent and which the dependent levels of description.

DVLPMNTS IN LANGUAGE TESTING
ISBN: 0-12-360880-5

Which point of entry then, the linguistic or the communicative, is the "true" one? The solution lies in the answer to two basic questions:

1. Is the theoretical basis of the particular approach well structured, coherent, credible and authenticated by systematically collected data?
2. Is the testing system devised in terms of the theory a logical realization of that theory?

It is my belief, and my major plea to my readers to consider, that at present there is *no* closely worked-out theory, or realization of that theory, sufficiently supported by data either to condemn one approach or to commend the other. The protagonists are thus in the same intellectual boat and it seems to me to be prudent for us all to pull together to reach our destination.

My own feeling is that a comprehensive and detailed specification of both communicative and linguistic fields is more likely to lead to a valid test than would a specification in one field alone and that tests (such as the new ELTS, RSA and SHAPE tests) in so far as they are realizations of the communicative specifications, are likely in that respect to be "better" tests. But, in fact, the making of these tests has been an act of faith, a decision urgently in need of scientific authentification by recognized validation procedures. The current verdict on the issue, then, must remain "not proven".

Support for the linguistic approach

To support the linguistic point of entry we can adduce these considerations:

The basic patterns of a language are well known, well described and essential to *all* forms of linguistic communication; the general plural form, for example, entails the addition of -s to the singular form (pen*s*), with exceptionally -en (child*en*) or zero (fish). There is no reason for ignoring these general patterns.

The correlation between different language tests is invariably high, and factor analyses invariably produce a large "g" factor accounting for much of the total variance. There is no reason merely to proliferate tests which appear to be measuring much the same thing.

Certain tests formats (some would exemplify the cloze and dictation procedures) are particularly useful in tapping general language proficiency regardless of the specific features of the differing linguistic situations.

The linguistic criteria for judging the correctness or acceptability are clear and widely accepted.

Therefore, why should we throw away such a clear, well known, generally accepted basis of testing for new, untried methods?

Support for the communicative approach

Communicative considerations would be:

The value of an interactive transaction lies ultimately in the appropriacy of the linguistic, or language-related, response and not primarily in its conformity to a particular language pattern.

The significance of an utterance varies according to its position in a text and on that text's position in an interaction.

There are many possible linguistic solutions to any interactional equation; language forms are resultants, determined by the purpose and strategies of an interaction.

Clear criteria for accuracy and appropriacy can only be found in the context of an identified setting and cannot always be gained on linguistic grounds alone.

Therefore the selection of language items and the judgement of their appropriacy must depend on a superordinate knowledge of the situational and fractional features of an interaction.

Areas of justification for testing language for Specific Purposes

Within the general caveat, already made, that there is no leakproof, authenticated theory to establish the superiority of communicative (or any other type of) testing, we can look for justification of specific-purpose language testing in a number of areas:

The recent Bachman-Palmer study, as presented at TESOL 1981, adds support to the existence of both a *general* factor of language competence and sizeable *specific* factors (grammatical, pragmatic and socio-linguistic) which is not too easy to ignore.

The dynamic relationship between language learning programmes and language tests obliges us to apply wider, educational considerations to the evaluation of tests such that their nature is not to be decided entirely by scientific (or certainly pseudo-scientific) considerations.

Tests must of themselves appeal to the testees as both human and worthwhile, and will be the better if they incorporate the characteristics of language as it is used from day to day.

Those who make decisions based on information from language tests will be the better guided and motivated if they can see in the test features which they themselves see in the jobs being tested for.

Thus there are a number of considerations—psychometric, linguistic and educational—which make the devising of specific purpose tests a reasonable, indeed promising, course of action. In such a situation, it is not imprudent to go ahead with such tests in the reasonable belief that data for operational and theoretical validation will become available in due course. The nettle is to be grasped by someone!

Parameters for specification

On the assumption that prespecification is a reasonable course of action, even in advance of firm theoretical or scientific evidence, then we have to examine on what parameters such a specification might be based. I believe they should include:

1. The range of levels of linguistic competence of the testees.
2. The nature of the personal interaction likely to be involved.
3. The nature and degree of the communicative needs to be experienced.
4. The content and focuses of the relevant job or discipline.
5. The job skills to be required, in terms of listening, speaking, reading and writing (in collaboration one with the other) as well as the language micro-skills concerned.
6. The essential job-functions, notions and concepts.
7. The language content in semantic and lexical terms.

The degree of specification

If we are to consider in our specification such an array of social, linguistic, occupational, functional and skill parameters, to what degree of specification should we operate?

Here, obviously, practical considerations must operate and we will have to be able to discern whether our decision is functionally critical, or merely cosmetic. For example, would we need a separate test battery for nurses and ward orderlies; or for the different branches of engineering—chemical, civil, electronic and mechanical; or for traffic and criminal investigation police? Probably the answer will lie in a complex of practical and theoretical considerations.

For one thing, the different labels given to jobs or disciplinary courses may not imply that they impose quite different demands, say, in terms of functions and language skills. And jobs within the same occupational area may involve quite different types of interaction. The categorization of job must then be very carefully carried out according to the selected parameters and the principles for establishing the degree of specification. Quite frankly, we are only at the fringes of such matters. However, I feel that if we can at least arrive at formulating the right questions we may ultimately arrive at composing the right answers.

Considerations for test construction

1. In the absence of a completely worked out theory for test design, there is much to be said for a general precept to incorporate into the test setting as many features as can be economically employed of the settings being tested for—the general principle of "replication".

2. The long standing and now largely rusticated dispute about discrete and integrative testing is by-passed in communicative test design where there *are* no discrete items, because all items are either directly or hierarchically related by virtue of their occurrence in a highly cohesive specification. The occurrence of a "discrete" item would be in violation of the basic test specification.

3. The relative importance of criterion- and norm-referenced procedures for the analysis of items has been a fruitful source of confusion in recent discussions. The universal question in all testing is whether, or to what extent, a testee can perform certain tasks, *not* where he is ranked in relation to his peers. The latter question can be answered if we know the answer to the former—but not vice versa. Norm-referencing is essentially tautological. Criterion-referencing is essentially radical. There can be no escaping the dilemma by conflating the essentially disparate nature of the two measuring procedures, or by asserting that criterion-referencing is a type of norm-referencing.

4. Perhaps the most disconcerting scientific finding of recent years as regards the testing of human, including linguistic, behaviour is that which comes from convergent-discriminant analysis studies. In short, it appears that a major feature that has been measured by language tests has been *the ability to do language tests*. The artefacts of testing have dominated the actual traits of linguistic ability—another point in the case for the principle of replication.

5. For many years the "educated native speaker" has been the criterion person for descriptions of the ultimate measure of linguistic competence. But once occupational and academic performance criteria are introduced, it is not tenable to continue with this general criterion. I know an Honours English graduate with some distinction as a writer and teacher who has been in tears because she could not understand one sentence of a treatise on nuclear physics—Band 1 on a 1 to 9 scale of proficiency! Any reasonably sophisticated L2 physicist would have handled the text without hesitation. The concept of the native speaker criterion person—inaccurate, invidious and unhelpful—is in urgent need of revision in the LSP context.

6. Above all, the statistics of probability, based on chance probabilities of independent occurrences, is largely irrelevant to a testing system where the test tasks and sub-tasks are consciously related at the design stage (e.g.

the Kuder-Richardson formulae require the independence of items). Similarly, the results of a factor or principal component analysis (as Ulrich Raatz has exemplified) can be manipulated towards a particular conclusion by the adoption of particular procedural options at various critical stages in the analysis, especially as regards decisions about rotation.

Thus, when the new theory of testing has been enunciated and substantiated by data, it is likely to be accompanied by a newly worked-out set of testing and statistical procedures.

Conclusion: Basic questions on specific purpose testing

1. How far is it true to say that the issues and procedures for devising specific purpose tests have been clarified?

2. Are there two major and differing points of entry to language test construction? (The "linguistic" and "communicative"; or other?)

3. Are the theoretical and operational justifications for the linguistic-structuralist approach to language testing satisfactory?

4. Has the attempt to grasp the nettle of communicative testing (e.g. ELTS) been premature?

5. Is LSP testing a category of communicative testing?

6. What considerations must be borne in mind in deciding (a) whether to devise specific purpose tests at all, and (b) how specific the specificity process should be?

7. What test construction and statistical procedural changes may be involved in specific purpose testing?

12

Response to Carroll

Some comments on "issues"

Keith Morrow

The stated aim of this paper is "to present some of the issues which have to be identified and clarified in the process of devising tests which attempt to incorporate systematically non-linguistic features of the job or discipline for which the tests were being prepared". Two obvious approaches thus suggest themselves in the consideration of the author's views: one is to look at the issues raised by the author and to comment on his treatment of them; the other is to focus quite specifically on issues which are not raised by the author in an attempt to highlight areas which would otherwise go by default. It is perhaps an interesting comment on this paper that I feel my most useful contribution will be to follow predominantly the first approach.

One of the most interesting issues contained in this paper is raised—implicitly—right at the beginning. Test constructors must always have a clear notion of what it is that they are attempting to test, and a test constructor working in the field of Language for Specific Purposes (LSP) is soon aware that from this perspective control of language *qua* language is a relatively unhelpful area to test. What is important is the ability to use language to perform various tasks. But the performance of these tasks will involve skills and processes far outside the area of interest of formal language study, or indeed (arguably) of any formal study at all. What then are we trying to test? Certainly not just knowledge of language; Carroll talks of "tests of linguistic behaviour", but am I alone in feeling that this obscures the problem? To me, the important point to make is that an LSP test can only be valid if it goes right outside language itself. It must be a test of performance of specified behaviours, but to call these "linguistic" behaviour does not help me because I am not sure what [a] "linguistic"

DVLPMNTS IN LANGUAGE TESTING
ISBN: 0-12-360880-5

behaviour is, and it might be (if I didn't know better) something as trivial as pronouncing "sawing", with an intrusive /r/.

It may seem to some that this is mere terminological quibbling. But one of the most obvious and significant differences between an approach to language teaching and testing based on "use" and one based on "usage"[1] lies in the status of language itself. For the former, language is a means to an end; for the latter, language is the end. A fundamental question for language testers is to decide from which end to start.

The first section of Carroll's paper suggests that the two "ends" outlined above represent "alternative approaches to language testing". He then discusses how we might decide which is the "true one". While I would obviously accept that there are two approaches, that a test constructor must choose one or the other, and that therefore they are alternative, I would argue that the choice is an illusory one, that it never really exists. Similarly, I would reject any suggestion that either can ever be characterized as the "true" one, and the other as a false idol. For what we are considering are not alternative versions of the same thing; rather they are chalk and cheese. Each is fitted for its own purpose, but it is not easy to write on a blackboard with a piece of Stilton. The question as to which is better resolves itself simply into a question of what each is to be used for. Taking this view means that one is led to reject the comforting and conciliatory claim in Carroll's paper that "the final products. . . . (of these approaches) . . . need not be of entirely different natures". Perhaps they *may* not, but I do not find the auctioneering example convincing. "Items to test the mastery of plural and comparison forms" should not find their way into a true performance test. There may be grounds for arguing that in a specific case a true performance test is not what is required and that a hybrid test containing performance and language competence elements (in Carroll's terms "communicative" and "linguistic" elements) is called for. But that is a question of purpose. If you want to make a sandwich of chalk and cheese, you can, but in doing so you are not making either of them more like the other.

Comfortable though questionable assumptions also seem to underlie Carroll's urging that new "communicative" tests (such as ELTS, RSA and SHAPE) are "in need of scientific authentification by recognized validation procedures". "Indeed so" we mutter approvingly, but what does it mean? Where are these "recognized validation procedures" waiting to spring into action? It would be very nice if we could offer "scientific" proof that these new tests are valid, but it is not at all clear to me what form such proof would take. Only construct validity could be investigated quantitatively (and even that only on the basis of often arbitrary assignment of questions/items in the test to categories derived from the theoretical model); concurrent validity in terms of existing "linguistic" tests should not be expected (though it may be found—but that is another story); and even predictive validity is a concept fraught with difficulty if one attempts to "prove" it convincingly. My feeling at this stage is that we may have to face up to the fact that performance ("communicative") tests must remain an act of faith, but that their great virtue will reside in that extremely unscientific concept, "face" validity. I would therefore endorse totally Carroll's later remark (which seems largely to contradict what he seems to be looking for here) that ". . . (we should) apply wider, educational considerations to the evaluation of tests such that their nature is not to be decided entirely by scientific (or certainly pseudo-scientific) considerations" [page 111]. From my own point of view as someone whose principal interest in testing relates to its backwash effect upon teaching, this is a vital consideration.

What is perhaps the heart of Carroll's paper is to be found in the sections on "Parameters for specification" and "The degree of specification". No prizes for seeing that the key issue here is "specification". Before considering briefly the particular points which Carroll makes, it is worth commenting that the dichotomy (real or imagined) between the desire to *specify* what performance is to be covered in a test, and the desire to *generalize* from the obviously and practically limited data provided by a test is implicit in much of the present heart-searching about the relative merits of "communicative" and "linguistic" tests. For a "communicative" test must specify. Inherently, it must focus on a specific communicative event or activity, where a specific set of features of a specific context of situation are delimited. Without such a delineation, the test cannot be communicative in terms of appropriacy. "Linguistic" tests, paradoxically, by focusing on the forms of the language in minimal or non-existent contexts, can claim generalizability to any context of situation, precisely because they measure it in none. Thus it is easier to extrapolate notions of proficiency from a "linguistic" test than from a "communicative" one. But it is important to note that Carroll goes one step further than this. He not only accepts without demur specification; he argues in favour of *pre*-specification. In doing so, it seems to me that he is moving right away from the notion of a proficiency test, and is accepting that a "communicative" test, based on a pre-specified set of parameters, is in fact an achievement test. The pre-specification represents a sort of syllabus[2]; what we are measuring is how well the learner can perform (how much he has achieved) in those particular terms. To say this is not to imply that this state of affairs is good or bad; but I think that it is true.

What then of the particular parameters of specification set out by Carroll in the section "Parameters for specification"? Without wishing to be snide or facetious, I don't know. I don't know because I don't know what many of them mean; I don't know, therefore, how internally consistent the list is; I don't know how exhaustive it is; crucially, I don't know how usable it is to generate tests that work. And that must be the most important factor, for it seems to me unlikely that this will be an area where so-called scientific rigour will in itself be of much use. The warning against the pitfalls of "pseudo-science" uttered above is even more applicable at this level of specification. History has already shown us one impressive looking, apparently rigorous, but ultimately unworkable model of needs specification[3], and we don't need any more. What we do need are tests that work for specified purposes in specified situations. Since the seven parameters specified by Carroll are unlikely to be equally relevant in all cases, and there is no indication of how in any general way we should attach priority to one over any other; and since there may be other parameters that are relevant in a given case (e.g. the general educational background of the candidates), it is clear that what we have here is one individual's checklist of parameters which seem to him useful. Since experience suggests that anything more "rigorous" is likely to be bogus or unwieldy or both, perhaps we should accept cheerfully that test construction in this area will always be more of an art than a science.

Turning briefly to the last section of Carroll's paper, "Considerations for test construction", I find it hard to plot a coherent path through the various points raised. They range from the academically interesting but ultimately fruitless ("Can discrete items exist in a communicative framework? What is discrete? What is integrated?", "When is a criterion a norm?", through the blindingly obvious ("replication is a good thing") to the genuinely interesting, ("the educated English speaker is not the ideal criterion in all situations", "we need to find new statistical procedures to substantiate developments in this area").

There is little to say about what is here; more to say about what is not. For the crucial problem in LSP test construction seems to me to avoid the charge that the final product is "interesting but trivial". Despite the acceptance that replication is a "good thing", we must not claim that any test can actually replicate reality, so the problem of sampling must be faced. In fact two problems arise. Firstly, what is the universe from which the test questions/items are drawn? This is a matter of the specifications and their relationship to the real world. Secondly, what is the status of the test items as samples rather than independent elements? This is a matter of the relationship between the questions/items in the test, and the specifications. Both of these must be dealt with satisfactorily if we are to give a convincing answer to the question: "What does it mean to pass your test?".

Raising this question brings me to the last part of my comments, where I want to consider briefly a potentially rather large area of which there is no mention in Carroll's paper: assessment.

Since one of the most frequently made claims for "communicative" tests is that they are performance based, and/or criterion referenced, it is interesting to ask ourselves what it means to "pass" or to get a score of x% on such a test. Presumably to pass means that the performance you have produced meets that criteria laid down. But it is unlikely that the test will consist of one "performance". There is likely to be a number of questions or tasks or items in the test and your overall performance is likely to be assessed quantitatively as a result of your performance on the separate elements. This is unremarkable as long as each element tests exactly the same thing; since this is most emphatically not the case in any real test of this sort that I know (for very good reasons), the procedure must be open to question. For if you score 6/10 in a 10-element test where each element tests something different, what criterion have you satisfied except a numerical one? Getting "questions" 1–6 right, and 7–10 wrong, will give the same result as getting 1–4 wrong and 5–10 right. But the "performance" involved will be very different. Unless we adopt a profile reporting system of a very detailed, and therefore unwieldly and probably impracticable type, I do not see a solution to this problem. But, as will be clear even from the over-simple example, I do see a problem.

Not the smallest merit of Carroll's paper is that it does not try to pretend that there are answers to all the problems. If occasionally one finds even problems which it does not mention, the omission should not be counted as a sin. I have enjoyed thinking through the issues that he has raised; who could ask for anything more?

Notes

1. This distinction is taken from Widdowson (1978).
2. I accept of course that this sort of specification is not a satisfactory teaching syllabus.
3. I refer to Munby (1978).

13

The effect of student background discipline on comprehension: a pilot study

J. Charles Alderson and A. H. Urquhart

In the testing of EFL reading proficiency, a major criterion in text selection has traditionally been that texts should not be subject-specific, but should be of "general interest". The aim of this is, of course, to avoid favouring any particular group. Among the assumptions underlying this approach would seem to be the following:

1. It is possible to identify "general" texts.
2. There exists a "general" reading ability which can be tested.
3. Following from the above, there is the assumption that the student who performs well on the general test will also be able to cope adequately with the subject-specific texts he encounters in his professional studies. Conversely, although the logic of this is questionable, it may be assumed that the student who has the ability to cope adequately with his subject-specific texts will also do well on general reading tests.

In the EFL field, at least, all these assumptions are open to criticism. It is arguable that there is no such thing as a general text in this sense, since what is general knowledge for one reader may be highly specific and esoteric for another. This is particularly the case with students from quite different cultures. The background knowledge needed to explicate a "general" text, which may be shared by large numbers of native speakers, may be quite alien to the student from another culture.

Secondly, we may be hesitant about accepting the existence of a general reading ability. While such a thing may certainly exist among educated

DVLPMNTS IN LANGUAGE TESTING
ISBN: 0-12-360880-5

native speakers who are exposed to a wide variety of texts, it is quite feasible to suggest than an L2 learner may have acquired much more specific skills for dealing with a far narrower range of text types.

We may then query both parts of assumption 3: the person successful on the "general" text may be from a group who find such texts particularly suited to them. There is a suspicion that "general" texts may favour readers from a Liberal Arts background. On the other hand, the L2 student may have acquired a competence in reading texts related to his subject area without being able to display this competence towards "general" texts.

Recently, there have been attempts, associated in the U.K. particularly with ELTS, to develop tests more related to the target subject discipline of the test-takers. This development merely reflects changes in language teaching practice towards specific purpose teaching, ESP. The assumption behind this development appears to be that it is more valid to test, say, an engineer's comprehension ability on an engineering topic, than on a general topic, and so on for physical scientists, medical students, etc.

As far as the practical problems of testing are concerned, there is no doubt that the traditional view of text selection presents far fewer difficulties. Subject-specific tests require a large number of tests, the number depending on how specific the test is required to be, e.g. do we have a test for all engineers, or one for chemical engineers, etc? Another problem is that of cross-disciplinary studies. If the ESP test contains at least three modules—Law, Economics, and Technology—and a student wishes to study Urban Studies, with classes in Law, Economics, and Technology, which module should the student take? Problems like these are not, on the whole, encountered with "general" tests.

Should, however, it be found that "general" tests were discriminating against a major group, say engineers, or that they were instrumental in denying further study in this country to students who were, in fact, quite competent readers in their own area, then clearly these practical advantages would not be enough to ensure the survival of general tests. The decision thus rests on empirical evidence, yet so far, empirical evidence in favour of either the general or the specific approach has been lacking. In the rest of this paper, we report on an on-going pilot study which was designed to gather such empirical evidence.

We hypothesized that students reading texts in a familiar content area, that is, related to their area of study, would perform better than students unfamiliar with that subject. The latter, it could be argued, might lack familiarity not only with the content of the subject area, but also with such aspects as genre effect, rhetorical organization, and linguistic and non-linguistic relations.

Design of the study

Four groups of students from a variety of language backgrounds and from different academic disciplines were tested at Aston University at the end of a pre-sessional English and Study Skills course. The groups were as follows:

1. Fifteen students about to do courses in either Development Administration or Development Finance. With one exception, all had practical experience in Administration or Finance. Most had first degrees in Economics.
2. Eleven engineers, about to study in a variety of post-graduate engineering areas, e.g. Chemical, Civil, and Electrical Engineering. All had a first degree in Engineering.
3. Six post-graduate students of Maths and/or Physics.
4. Five Arts and Social Science students, whose first degrees included Education (2), Psychology (1), and Language and Linguistics (1).

At the beginning of the English and Study Skills course, all the above students had taken a 100-item pseudo-random cloze test, consisting of a series of short passages on topics which in the opinion of the investigators showed no specialist bias. Results of this test may be taken as a rough guide as to subjects' linguistic proficiency and/or ability to complete a cloze task. Taking as correct only exact replacement of the deleted word, mean scores were as follows:

Table 13·1 Mean scores on test with no specialist bias

Group	1	2	3	4
Score	48.2	48.8	46.0	57.4

It can be seen that on this measure, the first three groups were virtually equal. Group 4, the Arts/Social Science group, were rather more proficient.

Five texts were selected. Two were on engineering topics, of which one, dubbed "Electrolytes", was from an academic monograph (Gregory, 1972), and the other, "Turbines", from an engineering periodical (Hulme, 1981). Two texts related to economic development and finance, "Polanyi" and "Investment", and were taken from the same university textbook (Latham, 1978). The fifth text, Quixote, designed to be the "general" text, was taken from the top level of the SRA 3B Ratebuilder cards, intended, according to the publishers, for native-speaker American junior-high and high school students (Science Research Associates, 1963).

From each text lexical items were deleted which, in the judgement of the authors of this study, were restorable from information in the text, i.e. their restoration was not intended to depend on students' knowledge of the content area. Particular attention was paid to the selection of items whose restoration depended on understanding of the text as a whole, rather than short chunks of language. (In the case of the "Investment" and "Electrolytes" texts, the text as a whole included tables and diagrams associated with the linguistic text.)

Example

At first sight, the pattern of investment in the Straits Settlements and Malay States appears to differ markedly from that in India and Ceylon. For there . . . . attracted the biggest proportion of British capital in 1910, ... 49 per cent. But the sum involved, £10.6 . . . . , was not much more than . . . . the £4.6 million invested in rubber in India and . . . . Apart from this, 36 per cent was in . . . . , most of which was spent on the substantial dock works of Penang and Singapore, and also on railways, although the . . . . current revenues of the Government . . . . . .

Extract from "Investment" passage

All texts were scored twice, once taking only exact word replacement as correct, then accepting any word which in the judgement of the investigators was suitable in the overall context.

Results

Mean exact word and acceptable word scores are presented in Table 13·2 together with the ranking of passages for each group on each scoring method.

Comments

1. The Engineers as a group performed better on engineering texts than Administration/Finance students:

Exact word:	"Turbines"	35.9 versus 34.3	
	"Electrolytes"	32.7 versus 20.4	
Acceptable word:	"Turbines"	54.1 versus 44.0	
	"Electrolytes"	52.1 versus 34.2	

Table 13·2 Mean scores and rankings on each passage for each group by each scoring method

| | Economics | | | | Engineering | | | | General | | |
| | Polyanyi | | Investment | | Turbines | | Electrolytes | | Quixote | | |
Group	Exact	Accept	Exact	Accept	Exact	Accept	Exact	Accept	Exact	Accept	n
Development administration/finance	13.2	42.7	29.4	44.7	34.3	44.0	20.4	34.2	12.2	33.3	15
Rank	4	3	2	1	1	2	3	4	5	5	
Engineers	8.7	19.0	25.1	34.2	35.9	54.1	32.7	52.1	7.0	22.5	11
Rank	4	5	3	3	1	1	2	2	5	4	
Maths/physics	6.1	21.2	23.5	33.3	30.8	40.0	26.7	42.2	14.7	22.5	6
Rank	5	5	3	3	1	2	2	1	4	4	
Arts/social sciences	15.5	38.2	28.2	34.1	38.0	49.0	26.7	36.0	14.1	30.6	5
Rank	4	2	2	4	1	1	3	3	5	5	
Total	10.9	30.3	26.6	36.6	34.8	46.8	26.6	41.1	12.0	27.2	37
Rank	5	4	2	3	1	1	2	2	4	5	

2. Administration/Finance students performed better on administration/ finance texts than the Engineers:

Exact word:	"Polyani"	13.2 versus 8.7
	"Investment"	29.4 versus 25.1
Acceptable word:	"Polyani"	42.7 versus 19.0
	"Investment"	44.7 versus 34.2

3. It is noticeable from the above scores that the effect of acceptable word scoring is to *increase* the differences between the groups.

4. It was not the case that the Administrators always found the administration texts easier than other texts. On exact word scores, they found "Turbines" the easiest text of all. On acceptable word scoring, "Turbines" was the second easiest text, easier than "Polanyi".

5. For Engineers, however, the two engineering texts, "Turbines" and "Electrolytes", were easiest, by both forms of scoring. This was also true for the Maths/Physics group.

6. For all groups, "Turbines" was the easiest text on exact word scoring. This may be because items tended to be restorable from the immediate context.

7. The most difficult texts were "Quixote" and "Polanyi", which the Engineers and Maths-Physics group found particularly difficult. The "Quixote" text, however, is possibly most typical of texts used for general texts and textbooks. On the basis of the results here, such texts should discriminate particularly against engineers, and maths/physics students.

8. The Arts/Social Science students perform similarly on all texts to the administrators, although (as expected) the Administrators had a slight advantage on administration texts. The Arts/Social Science group performed better than the Administrators on engineering texts. This may well have been due to their superior linguistic proficiency (see Table 13·1).

9. As expected, the Arts/Social Science group did better than the Engineers on non-engineering texts. However, in spite of their linguistic superiority (see Table 13·1) they did worse than the Engineers on engineering texts.

Conclusions

The hypothesis was supported that students from a particular discipline would perform better on tests based on texts taken from their own subject discipline than would students from other disciplines. That is, students appear to be advantaged by taking a test on a text in a familiar content area.

For Science students in particular—Engineering and Maths/Physics—tests in "familiar" content areas were easier than tests in unfamiliar areas. It should perhaps be noted that on the basis of the limited results presented above, Engineering and Maths/Physics students can perhaps be regarded as forming two closely related groups. Should wider testing confirm this, it would seem to have relevance for answering the question as to how specialized tests should be.

The Administrators, however, at times showed themselves capable of dealing more efficiently with a non-administration text than an administration one ("Turbines" versus "Polanyi"). This could be because the test task did not require discourse processing so much as the processing of smaller linguistic units, thereby calling less upon the subjects' background knowledge and experience.

Limitations and further research

Clearly this was only a small pilot study, and requires replication with larger numbers, which would render meaningful an examination of statistically significant differences between mean scores. Apart from this, the following directions for research suggest themselves:

1. Analysis of responses to cloze filling may shed indirect light on what students do to complete the blanks, and what the relationship might be between this and familiarity of content.

2. There is a need to investigate the use of different types of test task. At the moment we do not know if *different* abilities are measured or engaged by tasks in familiar content areas, or whether the *same* ability is measured better (or worse). It may be that a fundamentally text-oriented task like cloze favours Arts/Social Science students.

3. We might investigate readers' behaviour by using introspective and retrospective reports by individuals. This might shed light on the textual and non-textual information they use and what knowledge systems are brought into play.

It is clear from the above that further, more-detailed study of this area is required. What this pilot study shows, so far at least, is that there is indeed a relationship between content familiarity and test performance. This is particularly important, it seems to us, with the advent of ESP tests. If differentiated tests, such as ELTS, are to be established, then the effect of content familiarity needs to be determined. If general tests are to be developed across discipline boundaries, then equally the performance of students from different academic backgrounds with different academic targets also needs to be investigated.

14

The English Language Testing Service (ELTS): two issues in the design of the new "non-academic module"

Ian Seaton

The English Language Testing Service (ELTS) is operated jointly by the British Council and the University of Cambridge Local Examinations Syndicate to assess the language ability of overseas students and trainees who come to the U.K. for tertiary education. It is best described as an ESP proficiency test with a battery of five sub-tests accounting for language and language study skills in the main modes of communication. Results are reported in bands, 1–9 levels of ability; an overall band for proficiency and individual bands in the form of a profile for the sub-tests which can have a diagnostic use. There are, at the moment, six versions of the last three sub-tests, specific to five academic subject-areas: life sciences, medicine, physical sciences, social studies and technology, with one general academic version. These tests combine into modules and students take the one under which their proposed course of study can be classified.

There has, recently, been an increasing interest on the part of overseas governments and funding agencies in occupational, particularly technical, training in the U.K. ELTS has, therefore, in the last year or so been developing a series of tests, provisionally called the Non-Academic Module, to meet the need for assessing the language ability of this type of trainee and to complete the current battery. The language demands made on these trainees are different in type, level and content so the complete cycle of survey, content specification, test specification, test design and so on was begun. As ELTS is already administered in about 70 countries worldwide and is monitored centrally from London and Cambridge, the new module has also therefore to fit in with this system. Development has

DVLPMNTS IN LANGUAGE TESTING
ISBN: 0-12-360880-5

now reached the stage where two versions of the 3-test module are ready for pretesting. This account will look at two issues that were faced by those involved in the overall work; one from the stage of survey and one from the stage of test writing. If there is a common core linking the issues it is that of the need to make this module especially accessible and understandable in terms of its content and levels to those most affected by its operation: trainees and their EFL and subject teachers. And this bearing in mind that the module would have to provide, with its results, answers to the questions: can this trainee cope with the language demands of his course of training and if not what action is needed to ensure he/she can?

As with the academic modules of ELTS, the specification model used was that described in John Munby's "Communicative Syllabus Design" (1978) but it was decided to broaden the survey input to the specifications exercise with a questionnaire using terms more readily understood by trainers/teachers in colleges of Further Education and large companies or other bodies that offer on-site training to overseas students. The aim was to widen and substantiate the base for the more detailed specifications and to provide an overview and control of the appropriate weighting of sub-tests in the eventual module. The questionnaire was sent to a number of institutions and other bodies and some ten of the places that trained large numbers of such trainees were visited and the responses to the questionnaires validated, followed up and supplemented.

A copy of the questionnaire used is reproduced in Table 14·1; it follows a straightforward design in its five sections. The first four sections impose a framework which allows responses to be categorized and quantified to allow overall shapes to be perceived. The fifth section acts as the normal safety-valve in case the other sections are too prescriptive. The informant identification part at the beginning also allows an evaluation of the quality of response.

Section 1 controls the value of responses in Section 2 as well as gathering information on the relative "weight" of the three events most commonly encountered in training. Section 2 helps to establish a pattern of time, priority and difficulty for the component activities in each event. Section 3 uses the same three criteria but assigns them on the basis of mode to separate activities. It also requires a different type of response and allows comparison with responses in Section 2 to look at the internal reliability of the questionnaire. Section 4 is more self contained and serves a variety of purposes though less explicitly than the rest of the questionnaire; it allows the teachers/trainers to rank factors that they often immediately perceive as being "language problems", it gives an insight into differing tolerances of language inadequacy and it contributes to initial considerations of levels. Section 5 is particularly useful in trying to collect evidence on three perennial questions in ESP and English-medium study/training. Rubric for each section was kept to a minimum to avoid an intimidating clutter but for postal survey an ideally completed questionnaire with extra marginal notes was included for each place.

The analysis of completed questionnaires proved useful in allowing the specifier to test his own observation of particular trainees against the broader background and further down the line allowed the editing team a perspective in arriving at specifications to control the writing of items and tasks for the sub-tests. After pre-testing and during the actual operation of the module, the thinking behind this survey exercise will be used for longer term validation studies on the module to monitor the relationship between ELTS results prediction and actual performance in training.

The second issue, from the stage of test writing, was the definition and description of bands to guide the subjective assessment made in the third sub-test of the module (M3 Oral Interview), as well as to provide meaningful band descriptions for reporting results. The test specifications justified a longer M3 and a higher relative weighting in the overall band for this module than for the existing modules. This placed a greater burden on the test writers to ensure that the information provided by the interview was as reliable and valid as possible and allowed the users to understand what it all meant. Interviews pose particular problems of reliability and after several options were considered it was decided to divide the test into two parts to use two of the most frequent methods of scoring. The test specifications indicated the key language micro-skills and functions but tended to list these discretely without providing enough guidance in how to link them up in even a basic interaction. Again the design of two parts enabled lower-order skills to be considered separately in the first part while higher-order skills could emerge in the interaction during the second part. Users would require both "diagnostic" and "proficiency" information so the first part would emphasize the former, the second the latter.

Copies of the scoring grid and of the band description are reproduced in Tables 14·2 and 14·3 respectively. The grid is used in the first part of the interview to grade responses to the assessor's prescribed cue-questions (based on sets of language micro-skills from Munby's inventory). The task set is the operation of a simple cassette-recorder or transistor radio or towing bar for trailers for which a set of simple photos and diagrams is provided. There are three sets of cue-questions and the interaction during each set is expected to elicit performance to be assessed according to one of the three features listed on the left of the grid.

The band descriptions are used to assess performance in the second part of the interview which is based on a topic connected with either the trainee's work in his/her own country or his/her training plans in the U.K. There are no prescribed cues in this part and the performance is assessed as a whole following the description given for each band.

A tentative relationship between points out of nine and bands has been made but pretesting on a sample of some 400 should establish a firmer relationship. Thought is being given as to whether to make a correlational analysis of scores in the two parts and if so what, if any, inferences can be drawn from the result.

This account has covered, and then only lightly, only two issues in work that has involved a number of people for over a year. Further information and references to background material can be had from the ELTS Liaison Unit in the British Council, London.

Table 14·1. Survey for non-academic module: questionnaire

Institution/
Organisation .... Date ....

Programme .... Interviewer ....

T/S Name .... Position ....

Contact: years .... Hrs per week .... No. of students ....

1. In the settings below:	What time do students spend proportionately?	What is the order of importance?	What is the order of difficulty?
"Workshop" classes	☐	☐	☐
"Blackboard" classes	☐	☐	☐
"On site" attachments	☐	☐	☐
	100%		

2. In *"Workshop"* classes, with the activities below:	How many hours a week do students spend?	What is the order of importance?	What is the order of difficulty?
Listening (all) to demonstrations	☐	☐	☐
Solving problems/tasks	☐	☐	☐
Asking for information	☐	☐	☐
In discussion groups	☐	☐	☐
In one to one discussion	☐	☐	☐
Reading manuals/instructions	☐	☐	☐
Other activities	☐	☐	☐
....	☐	☐	☐

Table 14·1. continued.......

In "*Blackboard*" classes, with the activities below:	How many hours a week do students spend?	What is the order of importance?	What is the order of difficulty?
Listening to "lectures"	☐	☐	☐
In discussion groups	☐	☐	☐
In one to one discussion	☐	☐	☐
Asking for information	☐	☐	☐
Reading set texts	☐	☐	☐
Reading extra texts	☐	☐	☐
Solving problems/tasks	☐	☐	☐
Note taking	☐	☐	☐
Other activities	☐	☐	☐
....	☐	☐	☐

In "*On-site*" attachments with the activities below:	How many hours a week do students spend?	What is the order of importance?	What is the order of difficulty?
Following a "machinery" demonstration with Q/A	☐	☐	☐
"Machinery" observation	☐	☐	☐
Discussions with "teaching" staff	☐	☐	☐
Discussions with "non-teaching" staff	☐	☐	☐
Fact finding	☐	☐	☐
Reading manuals	☐	☐	☐
Notetaking/copying	☐	☐	☐
Organizing own schedule	☐	☐	☐
Socializing	☐	☐	☐
Other activities	☐	☐	☐
....	☐	☐	☐

Table 14·1. continued.......

3. Listening and speaking

Put the student activities below in "rank order" according to	How much time spent?	How important?	How difficult?
Oral reporting	☐	☐	☐
Group discussions	☐	☐	☐
Answering questions teacher–student	☐	☐	☐
Asking questions student–teacher	☐	☐	☐
student–student	☐	☐	☐
"Reading aloud"	☐	☐	☐
Other activities?	☐	☐	☐
....	☐	☐	☐

Are the questions asked usually for explanation or justification?
Are the exchanges usually simple Q/A or more developed with follow up?

Listening

Put the student activities below in "rank order" according to	How much time spent?	How important?	How difficult?
Listening while looking at source material	☐	☐	☐
Listening while following demonstration	☐	☐	☐
Listening with duplicated lecture notes	☐	☐	☐
Copying diagrams etc	☐	☐	☐
Copying dictations	☐	☐	☐
Other activities	☐	☐	☐
....	☐	☐	☐

Are students listening mainly to description/narrative or to instructions?
Are they listening usually for main points or for detailed information?

Table 14·1. continued.......

Reading

Put the student activities below in "rank order" according to	How much time spent?	How important?	How difficult?
Reading whole textbooks for "background"	☐	☐	☐
Reading parts of textbooks for particular information	☐	☐	☐
Reading duplicated notes	☐	☐	☐
Reading manuals/instructions	☐	☐	☐
Other activities	☐	☐	☐
....	☐	☐	☐

Are students reading mainly to answer set questions/write reports or for more general information?

Writing

Put the student activities below in "rank order" according to	How much time spent?	How important?	How difficult?
Extended writing (more than a paragraph)	☐	☐	☐
Writing restricted responses	☐	☐	☐
Writing short "connectors"	☐	☐	☐
Writing for exam preparation	☐	☐	☐
Other activities?	☐	☐	☐
....	☐	☐	☐

Table 14·1. continued.......

4.
Problems

Put the factors listed below in rank order according to how important you think they are in affecting students' performance.

Speaking		*Listening*	
Speed	☐	Speed	☐
Pronouncing	☐	Accent	☐
Grammar	☐	Selecting	☐
Vocabulary	☐	Grammar	☐
Shyness	☐	Vocabulary	☐
"Mistakes fear"	☐	Colloquialism	☐
"Entering"	☐	Other	☐
Other	☐		

Reading		*Writing*	
Speed	☐	Speed	☐
Skimming	☐	Expressing	☐
Scanning	☐	Organizing	☐
Selecting	☐	Grammar	☐
Grammar	☐	Vocabulary	☐
Vocabulary	☐	Spelling	☐
Other	☐	Layout	☐
		Other	☐

Table 14·1. continued.......

---

5. Comment: language as a factor in *overall* performance?
importance of social use of language (friends/pleasure)?
language tuition as preparation to programme?

....

....

....

....

....

....

....

....

....

....

....

....

....

....

....

....

....

....

....

....

....

....

....

Table 14.2 Scoring grid

	1 point (Inadequate)	2 points (Adequate)	3 points (More than adequate)
Accuracy	Grammatical and/or lexical errors in most utterances seriously interfere with communication	A number of errors in grammar, syntax and lexis, but these do not significantly interfere with the communication	Only occasional errors in grammar for syntax and very few lexical erros. No interference with communication
Range	Candidate uses only a very limited range of vocabulary, with frequent repetition. Nearly all simple sentences	Candidate occasionally lacks the appropriate vocabulary. Has difficulty in handling more complex sentence patterns	Candidate uses a range of vocabulary appropriate to the subject and shows ability to handle more complex sentence patterns
Clarity	Interlocutor has to concentrate very hard in order to under-stand the actual words spoken by the candidate	Interlocutor is aware of certain irregularities of pronunciation, stress and/or intonation which impose some strain on understanding	Interlocutor has no difficulty in under-standing the words spoken by the candidate. No serious problems with stress or intonation
	Bands 2–3	Bands 4–5	Bands 6–7

Table 14.3. Band descriptions of performance

Descriptions cover, in sequence, the features: Communicative Ability, Fluency, Flexibility, Appropriacy. The whole event, rather than the candidate's performance alone, is described.

Band	*Description*
7	*Good Speaker*: Communication is clearly and constantly maintained by fluent and well interconnected utterances with simple changes of topic easily handled. The interaction is appropriate to the context of the discussion and the intentions of the participants.
6	*Competent Speaker*: Communication is maintained with occasional breaks in the more complex exchange of meaning repaired by rephrasing; utterances are effectively interconnected although with a limited range of connectors; time is often needed to cope with changes of topic. The interaction is generally appropriate to the intentions and context of the discussion.
5	*Modest Speaker*: Communication is maintained but breaks in exchange of meaning often need repair by rephrasing; utterances are interconnected but with some effort and a restricted set of connectors; changes of topic have to be clearly marked and prepared for. The interaction is mostly appropriate to broad intentions and context of the discussion.
4	*Marginal Speaker*: Communication is limited to basic exchanges of meaning with utterances often incomplete and at slower speed with simple connectors; often confused by changes in topic as effort has to go into maintaining immediate topic. The interaction is mostly determined by the interviewer though stock phrases are used.
3	*Extremely Limited Speaker*: Communication is limited to simple questions and answers which often break down with slow and fragmentary utterances which focus on one basic topic at a time. The interaction wholly determined by interviewer.
2	*Intermittent Speaker*: No real communication other than isolated words and phrases. The interaction is barely sustained by the interviewer.

15

The validity of concurrent validation

Alan Davies

In publishing our validity information we are expected to indicate the levels for different forms of validity. In effect, this usually means that one statistical validity and one non-statistical validity are quoted, viz. either concurrent or predictive, and either content or construct. (It is, of course, the case that construct validity can be indicated, and increasingly has been in the literature, by Factor Analysis results, converting a non-statistical into a statistical validity.)

It is usually considered acceptable if one external and one internal validity are quoted.

A tenet that we learn early on in our language testing apprenticeship is the importance of the criterion and the desirability of the criterion being external. Whatever the elegance of internal structure, whatever the conviction of the claims to expert opinion, we still lean to the demands of objectivity. In testing, as Hughes reminds us (Alderson and Hughes, 1982), objectivity is demanded by the claims of reliability and validity. The external criterion, however hard to find and however difficult to operationalize and quantify, remains the best evidence of a test's validity. All other evidence, including reliability and the internal validities is eventually circular.

Let us consider first the special (but not uncommon) use of concurrent validity in validating a new test against an existing test. The explanations given for this procedure are of two kinds: the first is the cumbersome-simple contrast, viz there is an existing test but it is cumbersome, the new measure is simple or at least simpler and presumably not cumbersome, easier to apply and so on. The paradigm case is that of the Binet individual and group tests. The second reason is prediction-diagnosis relationship, viz. that while predictive validity has, as one would expect, to do with prediction, i.e. one uses it when the purpose of the initial test is to predict against a criterion separated from the predictor by time (always an unstated

DVLPMNTS IN LANGUAGE TESTING
ISBN: 0-12-360880-5

amount), concurrent validity is appealed to when the criterion measure is available at the same point in time. Since prediction is not at issue, what is being claimed is that if the test establishes concurrent validity then it is of diagnostic value, presumably in providing information that can be put to remedial use. In this scenario there is no need for either test to be a new one. It often is the case, however, that one is. In the examples Hughes quotes in his Epilogue (Alderson and Hughes, 1982) the new British Council ELTS instrument is necessarily being validated by predictive validity (because we do not have the criterion information present *now*), and the RSA Communicative Test of EFL is necessarily being validated by concurrent validity (because we are told by the RSA, no claim is made to prediction, but also, we can surmise, because we are concerned with communication *now*, not at some future point). I am not sure that I would wish to distinguish so rigidly between predictive and concurrent validity since for me the issue is largely practical in terms of when the criterion is available for observation and measurement. I see no reason in principle why ELTS (for example) should not be validated against a concurrent criterion of tutors' or supervisors' or teachers' scaled assessments *now*, nor why the RSA Communicative Test should not predict performance at some future date, e.g. performance (according to some agreed schedule) in an English speaking environment.

Next I want to consider some classical definitions of concurrent validity by Cronbach and Anastasi. They do not always agree. First the Cronbach.

In many situations for which tests are developed, some more cumbersome method of collecting information is already in use. If the existing method is considered useful for decision making, the first question in validation is whether the new test agrees with the present source of information. If they disagree, the test may have some value of its own, but it is certainly not a substitute for the original method. Validation again requires an empirical comparison. Both the test and the original procedure are applied to the same subjects, and the results are compared. . . . This type of empirical check on agreement is called concurrent validation, because the two sources of information are obtained at very nearly the same time.

The test constructor is not expected to answer every last question about validity before publishing his test, but he is expected to give the test user a fair impression of its validity.

Concurrent validity is investigated when the test is proposed as a substitute for some other information; this information is then the criterion. Designers of new tests frequently establish concurrent validity for their instruments by comparing them to established tests.

If a user needs a test badly, he may want to employ it for prediction even before the evidence on its predictive validity has been accumulated. Concurrent validity can be determined at once. The question to ask is: do test scores permit an estimate of a certain present performance?

(Cronbach, 1961)

Next the Anastasi: it will be obvious quite soon that I prefer her views to Cronbach's:

> The logical distinction between predictive and concurrent validity is based not on time but on the objectives of testing. Concurrent validity is relevant to tests employed for *diagnosis* of existing status, rather than prediction of future outcomes. The difference can be illustrated by asking: "Is S. neurotic?" (concurrent validity) and "Is S. likely to become neurotic?" (predictive validity).
>
> Correlations between a new test and previously available tests are frequently cited as evidence of validity. When the new test is an abbreviated or simplified form of a currently available test, the latter can properly be regarded as a criterion measure . . . . *unless the new test represents a simpler or shorter substitute for the earlier test, the use of the latter as a criterion is indefensible.*
>
> (Anastasi, 1961; my italics)

Anastasi goes on to make some interesting observations on construct validity.

> (Construct validity) has focused attention on the desirability of basing test construction on an explicitly recognised theoretical foundation . . . a possible danger in the application of construct validity is that it may open the way for subjective, unverified assertions about test validity. Since construct validity is such a broad and loosely defined concept, it has been widely misunderstood. Some textbook writers and test constructors seem to perceive it as content validity expressed in terms of psychological trait names. Hence they present as construct validity purely subjective accounts of what they believe (or hope) their test measures. It is also unfortunate that the chief exponents of construct validity have asserted that this type of validity "is involved whenever a test is to be interpreted as a measure of some attribute or quality which is not operationally defined" (Cronbach). Such a statement opens the door wider for fuzzy thinking about test scores and the traits they measure.
>
> Actually the theoretical construct, trait or behaviour domain measured by any test can be defined in terms of the operations performed in establishing the validity of the test. Such a definition would take into account the various criteria with which the test correlated significantly, as well as the conditions found to affect its scores and the groups differing significantly in such scores. These procedures are entirely in accord with the positive contributions made by the concept of construct validity. It would also seem desirable to retain the concept of the criterion in construct validity, not as a specific practical measure to be predicted, but more generally to refer to independently gathered *external data. The need to base all validation on data, rather than on armchair speculation, would thus be emphasised, as would the need for data external to the test scores themselves. Internal analysis of the test, through item-test correlations, factorial analyses of test items, etc., is never an adequate substitute for external validation.*
>
> (Anastasi, 1961; my italics)

Like others I have appealed for more work on construct validity (Davies, 1965). It is to be hoped that the present interest in construct validity (e.g. Oller, 1979) will establish itself as firmly as Anastasi recommends and not remain satisfied with the manipulations of correlations in terms of factor analysis.

I want now to report two results we have obtained recently. The first is an odd piece of flotsam which has just been turned up by chance and may therefore be spurious; but it may also be a kind of construct validity and therefore worth looking into further. The second result has to do with an orthodox concurrent validity analysis we are engaged in.

The first result comes out of our ELBA data (English Language Battery, Ingram, 1964) collected in Edinburgh over a number of years. The validation has proceeded in terms of two criteria, academic performance after one or more years, and tutors' assessments of language adequacy. When we look at ELBA scores for *satisfactory* and *unsatisfactory* language adequacy for certain mother tongue groups we find that the ELBA score that achieves a *satisfactory* language adequacy assessment for (e.g.) Farsi speakers is judged *unsatisfactory* for (e.g.) German speakers. Again, (e.g.) Icelandic and Nepali speakers are judged *unsatisfactory* at the score where (e.g.) Greek speakers are judged *satisfactory*. The numbers are not large and it may be a spurious result. But we will look to see if a similar curiosity occurs for the academic performance variable.

The more orthodox result comes out of the ELTS validation study we are currently undertaking. The experimental design is for ELTS, ELBA and EPTB (English Proficiency Test Battery, the former British Council test) to be administered to new students on arrival and for a repeat testing to be carried out in the early summer close to the final examinations, assessments etc. We hope thus to control for differential language learning over time and to maximize the "true" relation between language and content as indicated by the academic criteria. The second testing in relation to the academic criteria can be seen as one stage of concurrent validity. But in addition we have the initial stage of the three English tests. Here is straightforward concurrent validity. Or is it? Remember Anastasi . . "unless the new test represents a simpler or shorter substitute for the earlier test, the use of the latter as a criterion is indefensible". So perhaps we cannot call the ELTS–ELBA–EPTB comparison a means of establishing concurrent validity for anything, including ELTS, since in no sense do we have "a simpler or shorter substitute". No doubt what is a "simpler or shorter substitute" is open to interpretation, but as I understand Anastasi what she is arguing against is the validation of a test against its own parallel form. Such an incestuous proceeding is anathema to her as we see in her strictures about construct validity.

The result I have referred to comes out of an early pilot study in our ELTS investigation. A mixed (largely postgraduate) group of overseas students attending the Institute for Applied Language Studies, Edinburgh University, where they were taking a pre-sessional English course, were given all three English proficiency tests in September 1981. Spearman rank order correlation coefficients for the three tests are as follows:

	ELBA	:	EPTB	:	ELTS
ELBA	—		.92		.78
EPTB			—		.77
ELTS					—

(N = 30)

This is a very preliminary result which may not, of course, be confirmed. But as it stands it is a pleasing result, pleasing from different points of view. It indicates that ELBA and EPTB are quite similar and that ELTS is unlike both. But it also indicates that the *amount* of unlikeness of ELTS is not enormous (in that on this estimate ELBA and ELTS—or EPTB and ELTS—share about 60 per cent of the variance).

I conclude with another view of construct validity. My argument has been that we should be more attentive to concurrent validity and less enthusiastic about construct validity. In other words, external validation based on data is always to be preferred to armchair speculation.

16

The Associated Examining Board's test in English for academic purposes: an exercise in content validity

Cyril Weir

In pursuit of the communicative paradigm

It does seem necessary, before we can make any statements about the relative merits of direct as against indirect forms of testing, to develop valid and reliable, direct, communicative measures that effectively sample the domain we are interested in. For the moment then we are assuming that it is both desirable and feasible to evaluate samples of performance, in certain specific contexts of use, created under particular test constraints, for what they can tell us about a candidate's underlying competence. Having made this leap of faith it seems expedient to attempt to develop a framework of categories for description of the type described by Hawkey (1982), which would help us to identify the activities our target group are involved in, and to construct realistic and representative test tasks corresponding to these.

In the Test in English for Academic Purposes (TEAP) under development by the Associated Examining Board at Aldershot, we are fortunate in that we have been able to build on the earlier work of Hawkey (1982), Munby (1978) and Eggleston (1975). We have drawn upon their research in the construction of a framework of categories for the description of communicative test events: general descriptive parameters, dynamic communicative characteristics and task dimensions of target language behaviour. By applying these categories at the *a priori* test task validation stage we hope to avoid some of the problems which have arisen in some earlier efforts at communicative testing where no attempt was made to produce explicit specifications of the candidates' projected language needs

DVLPMNTS IN LANGUAGE TESTING
ISBN: 0-12-360880-5

in the target situation before test task construction took place. Though we would be cautious in claims for the directness of fit possible between test realization and specification, we would argue that this approach enables us to come closer to matching test tasks with appropriate activities in the target behaviour than would be possible using non-empirical approaches.

In order to pursue the communicative paradigm, tasks should as far as possible be included in the testing operation with due regard to their directness of fit with criteria which accurately and adequately describe the significant aspects of the target activities and the conditions under which they are normally performed. The concern is thus with content validity at the *a priori* stage as it no longer seems sufficient to rely solely on the more quantitative, *post hoc*, construct, predictive and concurrent validation studies to establish what it is that we have tested. Unless a communicative testing system is initially matched against such a framework, it is also difficult to see how we can ever get near to describing accurately the construct that we are attempting to measure. The more fully that we can describe the construct through our concern with content validity at the *a priori* stage, the more meaningful are the validation procedures that can subsequently be applied to the results of the test(s).

What follows (see Table 16·1) is a provisional attempt at such a framework of descriptive categories. It owes a lot to Munby (1978) in phase I, the General Descriptive Parameters of Communication, and a lot to Morrow (1977, 1979) in phase II, Dynamic Communicative Characteristics. For the most part though, the framework is derived from the work of Roger Hawkey (1982) particularly in phase III, Task Dimensions.

Table 16·1. Framework of categories for the description of communicative test events

General descriptive parameters of communication	Dynamic communicative characteristics	Task dimensions
Activities	Realistic context	Amount of communication involved
Setting	Relevant information gap	Grammatical complexity and range
Interactions	Intersubjectivity	of cohesion devices required
Instrumentality	Scope for development of	Functional range
Dialect	activity by participants	Referential range
Enabling skills	Allowance for self-monitoring by participants	
	Processing of appropriately sized input	
	Normal time constraints operative	

Establishing the general descriptive parameters of communication

The parameters established by Munby (1978), as part of his processing "model" for syllabus definition, are potentially of far greater use to the testers as a checklist against which they can evaluate the appropriacy of the performance based test tasks being developed. If the intention is to simulate in the testing situation those events and component activities students are faced with in the real world, then it is necessary to have a systematic basis for describing these. If we establish a set of general descriptive parameters applicable to events in the target situation these can then be used to evaluate the degree of similarity between the test tasks and the activities students are involved in, or are likely to be involved in, while operating in their real world situations. Additionally the set of descriptors provides a basis for comparing existing alternative test formats in terms of the appropriacy of the test tasks they involve vis à vis the situation the target population are likely to find themselves in. Unlike Munby (1978) we take activities as the first and most important parameter, for it is difficult to see how we can describe the other parameters before the activities participants are involved in have been established. We list below those parameters we feel it important to collect information on.

General descriptive parameters

1. *Activities*—i.e. the subtasks students have to cope with while participating in events, e.g. in a lecture situation a student might have to listen to the lecturer, take notes from the discourse, copy down dictation or notes from the board, read handouts, etc.
2. *Setting*—i.e. the physical and psychosocial contexts of the events, e.g. do students have to operate in the relative quiet of a lecture theatre and seminar room or in the noisier environment of a workshop?
3. *Interaction*—i.e. the role set and social relationships students are involved in, e.g. student–student, student–tutor.
4. *Instrumentality*—i.e. the medium, mode and channel of the activities within events, e.g. the activity of dictation would be characterised as spoken productive medium, monologue, spoken to be written mode and face to face (unilateral) channel.
5. *Dialect*—i.e. the dialects and accents the students are exposed to, e.g. R.P. (Received Pronunciation) or regional varieties.
6. *Enabling skills*—i.e. the underlying skills which appear to be necessary to enable students to operate in the various activities, e.g. in search reading to get information specifically required for assignments one might

identify component skills such as scanning for specifics or separating the essential from the nonessential in text.

As well as collecting data concerning the frequency of activities and the nature of attendant performance constraints that the target population have to cope with, we feel an additional focus for test design is provided by establishing the extent of difficulty overseas students experience in coping with these as compared with their native speaker counterparts. Where there is limited time available for testing, this might enable us to concentrate on those tasks which exhibit a high frequency of occurrence and where there is the greatest shortfall between the desired performance level and test population behaviour.

Establishing the dynamic communicative characteristics

In communicative approaches to language testing there would seem to be an emphasis not on linguistic accuracy, but on the ability to function effectively through language in particular settings and contexts. This involves the notion that linguistic activity in the tests should be of the kinds and under the conditions which approximate to real life (Kelly, 1978; Rea, 1978; Morrow, 1979; B. J. Carroll, 1980).

Davies (1978), adopting a minimalist position, argues that we need to do little more than ensure that we have a test of context as well as grammar, in the sense of making our test items more realistic. Rea (1978) takes a stronger line and argues the case for constructing tests that involve simulated communicative tasks which directly resemble those which testees would encounter in real life and which make realistic demands on them in terms of language performance behaviours.

The issue would seem to be whether there are in fact dimensions of language use that are not part of existing tests and which from a communicative perspective need to be incorporated, since it is important that testees are exposed to them.

If the communicative paradigm throws up these hitherto ignored features of language in use, a fundamental problem would still seem to exist in reconciling the realities of communication with the theoretical and practical requirements of assessment. The conditions for actual real life communication are not replicable in test situations which appear to be by necessity artificial and idealized and indeed must be so by virtue of their being set up. We would therefore agree with Davies about the illogicality of chasing the chimera of full authenticity, but would nevertheless argue that we should try and make our tests as realistic as possible in terms of the real life situation. For only if we try to make our test simulate as closely as possible the tasks students face in the academic context and the conditions under which these are normally performed, are we in a position to judge whether less direct measures of the same abilities can furnish us with similar evidence about student performance. It seems that we need to make our tests as direct as possible in the first instance in order to be able to compare the relative effectiveness of more traditional discrete point and integrative tests which are attempting to measure the same construct. It seems that in our communicative test we can at least achieve what Widdowson (1978:80) terms "authentic" language use, i.e. putting the learner in positions where he is "required to deal with . . . genuine instances of language use" in a way that corresponds to "his normal communicative activities".

If testers are committed to recreating as many of the conditions of real communication as is feasible in their tests, we agree with Hawkey (1982:164) that they need to be able to describe what happens "when the parameters of communicative events trigger each other off". While there are no definitive descriptions of such characteristics available, using Morrow (1977, 1979) and Hawkey (1982) and a small pilot survey as our major informing sources, we have attempted to list below a preliminary checklist of characteristics so far observed. No claim is made for the comprehensiveness of this list or that there is no overlap between categories. In addition some of the characteristics are more appropriate to one medium rather than another, e.g. intersubjectivity relates more clearly to oral interaction. It does seem to follow though that the more our test tasks reflect the dynamic communicative characteristics appropriate to target group activities then the more relevant the language behaviour that will result. Even if we are not able to incorporate all of these features into our tests for practical reasons, we still need some sort of yardstick whereby we can judge our own tests and compare them to other tests to see in what aspects they might be considered communicatively deficient.

Dynamic communicative characteristics

1. *Realistic context*—i.e. that test tasks are considered appropriate by candidates, e.g. as regards type of activity and subject matter. In the TEAP, listening and reading tasks are integrated with writing tasks as in an academic environment.

2. *Relevant information gap*—i.e. that candidates have to process not yet known information of a kind relevant to their real life situations and fill a similarly relevant gap for their interlocutor. In the TEAP oral component, for example, candidates will be asked to produce language in response to a variety of stimuli in contexts which correspond to those they might have to face in the academic environment.

3. *Intersubjectivity*—i.e. that the tasks involve candidates both as language receivers and language producers. In addition the language produced by the candidates should usually be modified in accordance with what their expectations of the addressee are perceived to be. In the TEAP candidates will be processing information from one medium to another in accordance with accepted academic conventions.

4. *Scope for development of activity by candidates*—i.e. that the tasks allow candidates the possibility of asserting their communicative independence. In the TEAP allowance is made for the creative unpredictability of communication in a number of the tasks set and in the marking schemes adopted.

5. *Allowance for selfmonitoring by candidates*—i.e. that the tasks allow candidates to use their discourse processing strategies to evaluate their own communicative effectiveness and make any necessary adjustments in the course of an event. In Session I of the TEAP, for example, candidates take notes while listening to a short lecture and are then given the opportunity to monitor these notes before writing them up in a note completion task. Sections of the notes revised for this task can then be used as a basis for part of an extended writing task.

6. *Processing of appropriately sized input*—i.e. that the size and scope of task activities are such that candidates are processing the kind of input that they would normally be expected to. In the TEAP both the written and spoken texts candidates are exposed to, are much longer than the texts candidates normally encounter in most other tests. For example, the reading passage in Session I will be about 2000 words in length and the lecture will last for about 8–10 minutes.

7. *Normal time constraints operative*—i.e. that the tasks are accomplished under normal time constraints. In the TEAP, for example, both the dictation and the lecture will only be heard once by the candidates and they will be expected to apply processing strategies just as in a normal academic environment.

Establishing the test task dimensions

Finally, we include below the part of the framework for describing the dimensions of particular events (Hawkey, 1982:166). This section of the framework serves two purposes. Firstly, it provides a description in more objective linguistic, stylistic terms whereby the target test task can be related more closely to the dimensions of the equivalent target language activity and, secondly, it enables the testers to plot their performance evaluation criteria against the dimensions inherent in the task itself.

Task Dimensions

Amount of communication involved	The amount of communication, receptive and/or productive that is involved in the event
Grammatical complexity and range of cohesion devices required	The degree of syntactic complexity, the range of cohesion devices (the overt relationships between propositions expressed through sentences) likely to be required
Functional range	The degree of variety of illocutionary acts involved in the event (coherence)
Referential range	The breadth and depth of lexical knowledge required to handle activities in the event.

Conclusion

It must be emphasized that this is a preliminary effort at establishing a Framework of Categories for the Description of Communicative Test Events and, as with nearly all attempts to break new ground, it will probably soon appear crude and inadequate.

It does, however, provide something concrete for people to react to and hopefully improve upon. Its value lies in the fact that though we might still be shooting in the dark with our language tests, at least we now have the possibility of spacing out our shots in a more systematic fashion.

Bibliography

Aborn, M., Rubenstein, H. and Sterling, T. D. (1959). "Sources of contextual constraint upon words in sentences." *Journal of Experimental Psychology* **57**, 171–180.

Ager, D. E. (1981). Review of Halliday, M. A. K. (1978). "Language as a social semiotic." *System* **9**, 66–67.

Alderson, J. C. (1979a). "The cloze procedure and proficiency in English as a foreign language." *TESOL Quarterly* **13**, 219–227.

Alderson, J. C. (1979b). "The effect on the cloze test of changes in deletion frequency." *Journal of Research in Reading* **2**, 108–119.

Alderson, J. C. and Hughes, A. Eds. (1982). "Issues in language testing." *ELT Documents* **111**, British Council, London.

Anastasi, A. (1961). "Psychological Testing", 2nd Edition. Macmillan, London.

Anderson, T. W. (1963). "Asymptotic theory for principal component." *Annals of Mathematical Statistics* **34**, 122–148.

Bachman, L. F. and Palmer, A. S. (1980). "The construct validation of the traits: 'communicative competence in speaking and communicative competence in reading'; a pilot study." Unpublished paper, presented at the Fourteenth Annual TESOL Convention, San Francisco.

Bachman, L. F. and Palmer, A. S. (1981). "The construct validation of the FSI Oral Interview." *Language Learning* **31**, 67–86.

Banks, B. (1981). "The Kent Mathematics Project." *The Institute of Mathematics and Its Applications* **17**, 48–50.

Beardsmore, H. B. and Renkin, A. (1971). "A test of spoken English." *IRAL* **9**, 1–11.

Bennett, S. and Bowers, D. (1976). "Multivariate techniques for social and behavioural sciences." Macmillan, London.

Bonheim, H. and Kreifelts, B. (1979). "Ein Universitätseingangstest für Neuphilologen." Universität, Cologne.

Botel, M., Dawkins, J. and Granowski, A. (1973). "A syntactic complexity formula." *In* "Assessment problems in reading." (W. H. MacGinitie, *Ed*). International Reading Association, Delaware.

Brière, E. J. (1972). "Are we really measuring proficiency with our foreign language tests?" *In* "Teaching English as second language." (H. B. Allen and R. K. Campbell, *Eds*.). McGraw Hill, New York.

Brown, S. (1980). "What do they know? A review of criterion-referenced assessment." HMSO, Edinburgh.

Burniston, C. (1968). "Creative oral assessment." Pergamon, Oxford.

Burt, M. K. and Dulay, H. C. *Eds*. (1975). "New directions in second language learning, teaching and bilingual education." TESOL, Washington, D.C.

Burton, N. G. and Licklider, J. C. R. (1955). "Long-range constraints in the statistical structure of printed English." *American Journal of Psychology* **68**, 650–653.

Campbell, D. T. and Fiske, D. N. (1967). "Convergent and discriminant validation by the multitrait-multimethod matrix." *In* "Principles of educational and psychological measurement." (W. A. Mehrens and R. L. Ebel, *Eds.*). Rand McNally, Chicago, Illinois.

Canale, M. (1983). "On some dimensions of language proficiency." *In* "Issues in language testing research." (J. W. Oller, Jr. *Ed.*). Newbury House, Rowley, Massachusets. (In press)

Canale, M. and Swain, M. (1980). "Theoretical bases of communicative approaches to second language teaching and testing." *Applied Linguistics* **1**, 1–47.

Carroll, B. J. (1978). "An English language testing service: specifications." British Council, London.

Carroll, B. J. (1980). "Testing communicative performance. An interim study." Pergamon, Oxford.

Carroll, J. B. (1958). "A factor analysis of two foreign language aptitude batteries." *Journal of General Psychology* **59**, 3–19.

Carroll, J. B. (1961). "Fundamental considerations in testing for English language proficiency of foreign students." *Testing*, Center for Applied Linguistics, Washington, D.C.

Carroll, J. B. (1968). "The psychology of language testing." *In* "Language testing symposium. A psychological approach." (A. Davies, *Ed.*). Oxford University Press, London.

Carroll, J. B. (1975). "The teaching of French as a foreign language in eight countries." Wiley and Almquist & Wiksell, New York and Stockholm.

Carroll, J. B. (1980). "Components and factors: complementary 'units' of analysis?" *Behavioural and Brain Sciences* **3**, 587–588.

Carroll, J. B. (1981). "Twenty-five years of research on foreign language aptitude." *In* "Individual differences and universals in language learning aptitude." (K. C. Diller, *Ed.*). Newbury House, Rowley, Massachussets. (In press)

Carroll, J. B. (1983). "Psychometric theory and language testing." *In* "Issues in language testing research." (J. W. Oller, Jr., *Ed.*) Newbury House, Rowley, Massachusetts. (In press)

Chihara, T., Oller, J. W. Jr., Weaver, K. and Chavez-Oller, M. A. (1977). "Are cloze items sensitive to constraints across sentences?" *Language Learning* **27**, 55–68.

Chomsky, N. (1980a). "Rules and representations." Columbia University Press, New York.

Chomsky, N. (1980b). "Rules and representations." (With open peer discussion and author's response). *Behavioural and Brain Sciences* **3**, 1–61.

Clark, J. (1980). 'Lothian region's project on graded levels of achievement in foreign language learning." *Modern Languages in Scotland* **19**, 61–74.

Clark, J. (1981). "Communication in the classroom." *Modern Languages in Scotland* **21/22**, 144–156.

Clifford, R. T. (1978). "Reliability and validity of language aspects contributing to oral proficiency of prospective teachers of German." *In* "Direct testing of speaking proficiency." (J. L. Clark, *Ed.*). ETS, Princeton, New Jersey.

Cohen, A. D. (1980). "Testing language ability in the classroom." Newbury House, Rowley, Massachussets.

Corder, S. P. (1981). "Error analysis and interlanguage." Oxford University Press, London.

Cronbach, L. J. (1961). "Essentials of psychological testing", 2nd Edition. Harper and Row, London.

Cummins, J. (1979). "Cognitive/academic language proficiency, linguistic interdependence, the optimum age question, and some other matters." *Working Papers in Bilingualism* **19**, 197–205.

Cummins, J. (1983). "Is academic achievement distinguishable from language proficiency?" *In* "Issues in language testing research." (J. W. Oller, Jr., *Ed.*). Newbury House, Rowley, Massachussets. (In press)

Davies, A. (1964). "English proficiency test battery. Version A." British Council, London.

Davies, A. (1965). "Proficiency in English as a second language. PhD Thesis, University of Birmingham.

Davies, A. (1978). "Language testing: survey article." *Language Teaching and Linguistics: Abstracts* **11**, 145–159, 215–231.

Davies, A. (1982). "Reaction to the Bachman & Palmer and the Vollmer papers." *In* "Issues in language testing." (J. C. Alderson and A. Hughes, *Eds.*). British Council, London.

Davies, A. and Allen, J. P. B. *Eds.* (1977). "Language and learning: The Edinburgh Course in Applied Linguistics, Vol. 4: testing and experimental methods." Oxford University Press, London.

Davis, R. (1977). "All protein and no roughage makes Hamid a constipated student." *In* "English for specific purposes." (S. Holden, *Ed.*). Modern English Publications, London.

Eastment, H. T. and Krzanowski, W. J. (1982). "Cross-validatory choice of the number of components from a principal components analysis." *Technometrics* **24**, 73–77.

Eggleston, J. F. (1975). "A science teaching observation schedule." Macmillan Educational, London.

English Language Teaching Development Unit, (no date). "Stages of attainment scale and test battery." ELTDU, Bicester.

English Speaking Board, (no date). "Syllabuses." English Speaking Board, Southport.

Faerch, C. and Kasper, G. (1980). "Processes and strategies in foreign language learning and communication." *Interlanguage Studies Bulletin* **5**, 47–118.

Farhady, H,. (forthcoming). "On the plausibility of the unitary language proficiency factor." *In* "Issues in language testing research." (J. W. Oller, Jr. *Ed.*). Newbury House, Rowley, Massachussets.

Felix, S. W. (1981). "On the (in)applicability of Piagetian thought to language learning." *Studies in Second Language Acquisition* **3**, 179–192.

Ferguson, N. (1980). "The Gordian Knot." CEEL, Geneva.

Fillenbaum, S., Jones, L. V. and Rapoport, A. (1963). "The predictability of words and their grammatical classes as a function of rate of deletion from a speech transcript." *Journal of Verbal Learning and Verbal Behaviour* **2**, 186–194.

Fischer, R. A. (1981). "The role of cyclicity in testing for linguistic competence and communicative competence in foreign language instruction." Unpublished paper given at 4th International Language Testing Symposium, University of Essex.

Fox, B. (1979). "Communicative competence and the APU." *Language for Learning (Exeter)* **1**, 159–167.

Gardner, R. C. and Lambert, W. E. (1965). "Language aptitude, intelligence, and second language learning." *Journal of Educational Psychology* **56**, 191–199.
Geddes, M. and Sturtridge, G. (1978). "Listening links." Heinemann, London.
Gregory, D. P. (1972). "Fuel cells." Mills and Boon, London.
Guttman, L. (1954). "Some necessary conditions for common-factor analaysis." *Psychometrica* **19**, 149–161.
Harding, A., Page, B. and Rowell, S. (1980). "Graded objectives in modern languages." CILT, London.
Harrison, A. (1979). "Techniques for evaluating a learner's ability to apply Threshold Level proficiency to everyday communication." Council of Europe, Strasbourg.
Harrison, A. (1980). "Current views on the Institute's examinations: extracts from the Examination Review report." *The Incorporated Linguist* **19**, 38–42.
Harrison, A. (1982). "Review of graded tests." Macmillan Educational, London.
Harrison. A. (1983). "A language testing handbook." Macmillan, London.
Hawkey, R. (1982). "An investigation of interrelationships between cognitive/ affective and social factors and language learning. A longitudinal study of twenty-seven overseas students using English in connection with their training in the United Kingdom." Unpublished Ph.D. thesis, University of London.
Hawkins, E. and Perren, G. E. (1978). "Intensive language teaching in schools." CILT, London.
Hayward, T., Michiels, A. and Noel, J. (1981). "An experiment in combining activation and testing techniques for advanced students." Unpublished paper, given at 4th International Language Testing Symposium, University of Essex.
Holden, S. *Ed*. (1977). "English for specific purposes." Modern English Publications, London.
Holtzman, P. (1967). "English language testing and the individual." *In* Selected conference papers of the Association of Teachers of English as a Second Language.
Horst, P. (1963). "Matrix algebra for social scientists." Holt, Reinhart and Winston, New York.
Hosley. D. and Meredith, K. (1979). "Inter- and intra-test correlates of the TOEFL. "*TESOL Quarterly* **13**, 209–217.
Hughes, A. (1979). "Aspects of a Spanish adult's acquisition of English." *Interlanguage Studies Bulletin* Utrecht, 4.
Hughes, A. and Woods, A. (1982). "Unitary competence and Cambridge Proficiency." *Journal of Applied Language Study* **1**, 5–15.
Hulme, B. G. (1981). "Development of off-shore gas-turbine packages for power generation and mechanical drive." *GEC Journal of Science and Technology* **47**.
Hunter, J. E. (1980). "Multivariate techniques in human communication research." *In* "Factor Analysis." (P. R. Monge and J. N. Cappella, *Eds*.). Academic Press, New York and London.
Ingram, E. (1964). "English Language Battery." Department of Linguistics, University of Edinburgh.
Institute of Linguists. (no date). "Syllabus of Examinations." IL, London.
Johns-Lewis, C. (1981). "Testing communicative competence." *MALS Journal*, Spring.

Johnstone, R. (1980). "An interim outline of the 'Tour de France' syllabus for first-year classes." *Modern Languages in Scotland* **19**, 34–50.

Jones, B. L. (1979). "Le jeu des colis—an exercise in foreign language communication." *Audio-Visual Language Journal* **17**, 159–167.

Jones, K. (1980). "Simulations—a handbook for teachers." Kogan Page, London.

Jones, R. L. and Spolsky, B. *Eds*. (1975). "Testing language proficiency." Center for Applied Linguistics, Arlington, Virginia.

Jupp, T. C. and Hodlin, S. (1975). "Industrial English." Heinemann, London.

Kelly, R. (1978). "On the construct validation of comprehension tests: an exercise in applied linguistics." PhD thesis, University of Queensland.

Kendall, M. (1980). "Multivariate analysis." Charles Griffin, London.

Klein-Braley, C. and Lück, H. E. (1979). "The development of the Duisburg English Language Test for Advanced Students (DELTA)." *In* "Empirical research on language teaching and language acquisition." (R. Grotjahn and E: Hopkins, *Eds*) Brockmeyer, Bochum.

Knox, J. D. E. (1975). "The modified essay question." Association for the Study of Medical Education, Dundee.

Landis, G. B. (1980). "Ideational exchange." *System* **8**. 157–158.

Latham, A. J. H. (1978). "The international economy and the underdeveloped world, 1864–1914." Croom Helm, London.

Lee, W. R. (1979). "Language teaching games and contests." Second edition. Oxford University Press, Oxford.

Löfgren, H. (1969). "Measuring proficiency in the German language: a study of pupils in grade 7." School of Education, Malmö.

Lompscher, J. (1972). "Theoretische und experimentelle Untersuchungen zur Entwicklung geistiger Tätigkeit." Volk und Wissen, Berlin.

Lompscher, J. (1976). "Verlaufsqualitäten der geistigen Tätigkeit." Volk und Wissen, Berlin.

Lynch, M. (1977). "It's your choice." Arnold, London.

MacGinitie, W. H. (1961). "Contextual constraint in English prose paragraphs." *Journal of Psychology* **51**, 121–130.

McLaughlin, B. (1980). "On the use of miniature artificial languages in second language research." *Applied Psycholinguistics* **1**, 357–369.

Maley, A. and Grellet, F. (1981). "Mind matters." Cambridge University Press, Cambridge.

Mandl, H. and Zimmerman, A. (1976). "Intelligenzdifferenzierung." Kohlhammer, Stuttgart.

Marriott, F. H. C. (1974). "The interpretation of multiple observations." Academic Press, New York and London.

Maxwell, A. E. (1977). "Multivariate analysis in behavioural research." Chapman and Hall, London.

Miller, G. A. and Isard, S. (1963). "Some perceptual consequences of linguistic rules." *Journal of Verbal Learning and Verbal Behaviour* **2**, 217–228.

Moore, J. *Ed*. (1980). "Reading and thinking in English: Discourse in action." Teacher's book. Oxford University Press, Oxford.

Morrison, D. F. (1976). "Multivariate statistical methods." 2nd edition. McGraw-Hill, New York and London.

Morrow, K. (1977). "Techniques of evaluation for a notional syllabus." Royal Society of Arts, London.

Morrow, K. (1979). 'Communicative language testing: revolution or evolution?" *In*

"The communicative approach to langauge teaching." (C. J. Brumfit and K. Johnson, *Eds.*). Oxford University Press, Oxford.

Munby, J. (1978). "Comunicative syllabus design." Cambridge University Press, Cambridge.

Neisser, U. (1967). "Cognitive psychology." Appleton-Century-Crofts, New York.

Neisser, U., (1976). "Cognition and reality." Freeman, San Francisco.

North West Regional Examinations Board. (1980). "English as a second language: notes for the guidance of teachers." NWREB, Manchester.

Nott, D. *Ed.* (1977). "Language teaching 16–19: a handbook." *Audio-Visual Language Journal.*

Oller, J. W., Jr. (1974). "Expectancy for successive elements: key ingredients to language use." *Foreign Language Annals* **7**, 443–452.

Oller, J. W., Jr. (1975). "Cloze, discourse and approximations to English." *In* Burt, M. K. and Dulay, H. C. *Eds.* (1975).

Oller, J. W., Jr. (1976). "Evidence for a general language proficiency factor: an expectancy grammar." *Die Neueren Sprachen* **75**, 165–174.

Oller, J. W., Jr. (1978). "Pragmatics and language testing." *In* "Approaches to language testing." (B. Spolsky, *Ed.*). Center for Applied Linguistics, Arlington, Virginia.

Oller, J. W., Jr. (1979). "Language tests at school." Longman, London.

Oller, J. W., Jr. (1980). "Language testing research." *In* "Annual Review of Applied Linguistics." (R. Kaplan, *Ed.*). Newbury House, Rowley, Massachussets.

Oller, J. W., Jr. (1981). "Language as intelligence?" *Language Learning* **31**, 465–492.

Oller, J. W., Jr., (1982). "Are we testing for intelligence or language?" *In* "Proceedings of the Second Annual Language Assessment Institute, June 1982." (S. S. Seidner, *Ed.*). Illinois State Board of Education, Chicago.

Oller, J. W., Jr. (1983a). "Episodic organization and language acquisition." *In* "Proceedings of the Fourth Annual Delaware Symposium on Language Studies." (S. Williams, *Ed.*). Ablex, Norwood, New Jersey. (In press)

Oller, J. W., Jr. (1983b). "Practical principles for language teaching and testing." *TESOL Quarterly.* (In press)

Oller, J. W., Jr. (1983c). "A concensus for the '80s?" *In* "Issues in language testing research." (J. W. Oller, Jr. *Ed.* (In press)

Oller, J. W., Jr. *Ed* (1983d). "Issues in language testing research." Newbury House, Rowley, Massachussets. (In press)

Oller, J. W., Jr. and Hinofotis, F. B. (1980). "Two mutually exclusive hypotheses about second language ability: indivisible or partially divisible competence." *In* "Research in language testing." (J. W. Oller, Jr. and K. Perkins, *Eds.*). Newbury House, Rowley, Massachussets.

Parkinson, B. L., McIntyre, D. I., Mitchell, R. F. and Nutt, A. D. (1983). "Report of the independent evaluation of 'Tour de France'." Department of Education, University of Stirling, Stirling. (In press)

Penrose, L. S. (1953). "The general purpose sib-pair linkage test." *Annals of Eugenics* **18**, 120–124.

Phillips, D. *Ed.* (1978). "Continuation German; report of the Oxford-BP German Project 1977–78." University of Oxford Department of Educational Studies, Oxford.

Pimsleur, P., Stockwell, R. P. and Comrey, A. L. (1962). "Foreign language learning ability." *Journal of Educational Psychology* **53**, 15–26.

Purcell, E. T. (1983). "Models of pronunciation accuracy." *In* "Issues in language testing research." (J. W. Oller, Jr.). (In press)

Raatz, U. (1980). "Language theory and factor analysis." *In* "Practice and problems in language testing, 3." (T. Culhane and M. Lutjeharms, *Eds.*). Vrije Universiteit, Brussels.

Rao, C. R. (1965). "Linear statistical inference and its applications." Wiley, New York.

Rea, P. M. (1978). "Assessing language as communication." *MALS Journal* New series, 3. University of Birmingham.

Royal Society of Arts, (1980). "Examinations in the communicative use of English as a foreign language; specifications and specimen papers." RSA, London.

Salzinger, K., Portnoy, S. and Feldman, R. S. (1962). "The effect of order of approximation to the statistical structure of English on the emission of verbal responses." *Journal of Experimental Psychology* 64, 52–57.

Sang, F. (forthcoming). "Die Struktur von Fremdsprachenleistungen unter dem Einfluss von Muttersprache, Intelligenz, Motivation und Lehrerbewertungen (Noten)." Max-Planck-Institut für Bildungsforschung, Berlin.

Sang, F. and Vollmer, H. J. (1978). "Allgemeine Sprachfähigkeit und Fremd-sprachenerwerb: zur Struktur von Leistungsdimensionen und linguistischer Kompetenz bei Fremdsprachenlernern." Max-Planck-Institut für Bildungs-forschung, Berlin.

Sang, F. and Vollmer, H. J. (1980). "Modelle linguistischer Kompetenz und ihre empirische Fundierung." *In* "Empirical research on language teaching and language acquisition." (R., Grotjahn and E. Hopkins, *Eds.*), Brockmeyer, Bochum. *Quantitative Linguistics* 6.

Scholz, G., Hendricks, D., Spurling, R., Johnson, M. and Vandenburg, L. (1980). "Is language ability divisible or unitary? A factor analysis of 22 English language proficiency tests." *In* "Research in language testing." (J. W. Oller, Jr. and K. Perkins, *Eds.*). Newbury House, Rowley, Massachussets.

Selinker, L. and Lamendella, J. T. (1981). "Updating the interlanguage hypo-thesis." *Studies in Second Language Acquisition* 3, 201–220.

Sewell, P. (1976). "Feedback and assessment." *In* "Teaching languages." (E. Baer, *Ed.*). BBC, London.

Shapira, R. G. (1978). "The non-learning of English: case study of an adult." *In* "Second language acquisition: a book of readings." (E. M. Hatch, *Ed.*). Newbury House, Rowley, Massachussets.

Shayer, M. and Adey, P. (1981). "Towards a science of science teaching." Hein-mann, London.

Snow, C. E. and Hoefnagel-Höhle, M. (1979). "Individual differences in second language ability: a factor analytic study." *Language and Speech* 22, 151–162.

Spearman, C. (1904). "The proof and measurement of association between two things." *Am. J. Psychol.* 15, 88–103.

Spolsky, B. (1967). "Do they know enough English? *In* "Selected Conference papers of the Association of teachers of English as a Second Language."

Spolsky, B. (1968). "Language testing—the problem of validation." *TESOL Quarterly* 2, 88–94.

Spolsky, B. (1971). "Reduced redundancy as a language testing tool." *In* "Appli-cations of linguistics." (G. E. Perren and J. L. M. Trim, *Eds*). Cambridge University Press, Cambridge.

Spolsky, B. (1973). "What does it mean to know a language, or how do you get someone to perform his competence ?" *In* "Focus on the Learner." (J. W. Oller, Jr. and J. C. Richards, *Eds.*). Newbury House, Rowley, Massachussets.

Spolsky, B. (1981). "Some ethical questions about language testing." *In* "Practice and problems in language testing, 1." (C. Klein-Braley and D. Stevenson, *Eds.*). Verlag Peter D. Lang, Bern and Frankfurt am Main.

Spolsky, B., Murphy, P., Holm, W. and Ferrel, A. (1972). "Three functional tests of oral proficiency." *TESOl Quarterly* **6**, 221–235.

Spolsky, B., Sigurd, B., Sato, M., Walker, E., and Aterburn, C. (1968). "Preliminary studies in the development of techniques for testing overall second language proficiency." *Language Learning* Special Issue **3**, 79–101.

Science Research Associates, (1963). "SRA Reading Laboratory." Science Research Associates, Inc., Chicago.

Stegelmann, W. (1980). "Theorie über Lösungen von Testaufgaben." Max-Planck-Institut für Bildungsforschung, Berlin.

Steltmann, K. (1979). "Faktoren der Fremdsprachenleistung." Kastellaun, Henn.

Sternberg, R. J. (1977). "Intelligence, information processing, and analogical reasoning: the componential analysis of human abilities." Erlbaum, Hillsdale, N.J.

Sternberg, R. J. (1980). "Sketch of a componential subtheory of human intelligence." *Behavioural and Brain Sciences* **4**, 573–614.

Stevenson, D. K. (1979). "Beyond faith and face validity." Unpublished paper presented at TESOL Colloquium, Boston.

Sturtridge, G. (1977). "Using simulation in teaching English for specific purposes." *In* "English for Specific Purposes." (S. Holden, *Ed.*). Modern English Publications.

Swanwick, K. (1981). "Towards a musical examination." Times Educational Supplement, 3rd April.

Tarone, E. E. (1979). "Interlanguage as chameleon." *Language Learning* **29**, 181–191.

Tough, J. (1973). "Talk for teaching and learning." Ward Lock Educational, London.

Trinity College of Music, (no date). Syllabuses of grade and diploma examinations. TCM, London.

Upshur, J. A. and Homburg, T. J. (1983). "Some relations among language tests at successive ability levels." *In* "Issues in language testing research." (J. W. Oller, Jr. *Ed.*). Newbury House, Rowley, Massachussets. (In press)

Valette, R. (1974). "Using classroom tests to improve instruction." *Audio-Visual Language Journal* **12**, 217–221.

Vigil, N. and Oller, J. W., Jr. (1976). "Rule fossilization: a tentative model." *Language learning* **26**, 281–295.

Vollmer, H. J. (1981a). "Why are we interested in 'General Language Proficiency'?" *In* "Practice and problems in language testing." (C. Klein–Braley and D. K. Stevenson, *Eds.*). Peter Lang Verlag, Bern and Frankfurt am Main.

Vollmer, H. J. (1981b). "Receptive versus productive competence? Models, findings, and psycholinguistic considerations in L2 testing." Unpublished paper, presented at the 6th AILA World Congress in Lund, Sweden.

Vollmer, H. J. (1982a). "Issue or non-issue? General Language Proficiency revisited—Author's response." *In* "Issues in language testing." (J. C. Alderson and A. Hughes, *Eds.*). British Council (ELT Documents 111), London.

Vollmer, H. J. (1982b). "Spracherwerb und Sprachbeherrschung: Untersuchungen zur Struktur von Fremdsprachenfähigkeit." Narr Verlag, Tübingen.

Vollmer, H. J. (forthcoming). "Kognitive Analyse und Probleme der Bewertung mündlicher Sprechhandlungen von Fremdsprachenlernern." In "Kongressberichte der 12. Jahrestagung der Gesellschaft für Angewandte Linguistik GAL e.V., Mainz 1981." (W. Kühlwein and A. Raasch, Eds.). Narr, Tübingen.

Vollmer, H. J. and Sang, F. (1980). "Zum psycholinguistischen Konstrukt einer internalisierten Erwartungsgrammatik." Linguistik und Didaktik 42, 122–148.

Vollmer, H. J. and Sang, F. (1983). "Competing hypotheses about second language ability: a plea for caution." In "Issues in language testing research." (J. W. Oller, Jr. Ed Newbury House, Rowley, Massachussets. (In press)

White, R. V. (1980). "Teaching written English." George Allen and Unwin, London.

Widdowson, H. G. (1978). "Teaching language as communication." Oxford University Press, Oxford.

Wright, A., Betteridge, B. and Buckby, M. "Games for language learning." Cambridge University Press, Cambridge.

Wright, D. W. (1980). "TEFL and ESP in French higher education: the case study and role-play approach." System 8, 103–111.

Wright, D. W. (1981). "Simulation and gaming in TEFL: resource list." Simulation/Games for Learning 11, 140–143.

Yorozuya, R. and Oller, J. W. (1980). "Oral plroficiency scales: construct validity and the halo effect." Language Learning 30, 135–153.

Index